Que® Quick Reference Series

MS-DOS Quick Reference

Developed by
Que® Corporation

Que® Corporation
Carmel, Indiana

Library of Congress Catalog No.: 88-61936

ISBN 0-88022-369-3

91 90   9 8 7

Interpretation of the printing code: the rightmost
double-digit number is the year of the book's printing;
the rightmost single-digit number, the number of the
book's printing. For example, a printing code of 87-4
shows that the fourth printing of the book occurred in
1987.

Based on MS-DOS Version 3.3 and the earlier versions
3.2, 3.1, and 3.0.

Que Quick Reference Series

The *Que Quick Reference Series* is a portable resource of essential microcomputer knowledge. Whether you are a new or experienced user, you can rely on the high-quality information contained in these convenient guides.

Drawing on the experience of many of Que's best-selling authors, the *Que Quick Reference Series* helps you easily access important program information. Now it's easy to look up often-used commands and functions for 1-2-3, WordPerfect 5, MS-DOS, and dBASE IV, as well as programming information for C and QuickBASIC 4.

Use the *Que Quick Reference Series* as a compact alternative to confusing and complicated traditional documentation.

The *Que Quick Reference Series* also includes these titles:

1-2-3 Quick Reference
1-2-3 Release 3 Quick Reference
Assembly Language Quick Reference
AutoCAD Quick Reference
C Quick Reference
dBASE IV Quick Reference
DOS and BIOS Functions Quick Reference
Hard Disk Quick Reference
Microsoft Word 5 Quick Reference
PC Tools Quick Reference
QuickBASIC Quick Reference
Turbo Pascal Quick Reference
WordPerfect Quick Reference

Publishing Director
Scott N. Flanders

Product Director
Karen A. Bluestein

Senior Editor
Lloyd J. Short

Editorial Assistant
Debra S. Reahard

Cover designed by
Listenberger Design Associates

Production
Composed on a Macintosh II using PageMaker 3.0

Trademark Acknowledgments
Macintosh is a registered trademark of Apple Computer, Inc.

MS-DOS is a registered trademark of Microsoft Corporation.

PageMaker is a registered trademark of Aldus Corporation.

ProKey is a trademark of RoseSoft, Inc.

SideKick is a registered trademark of Borland International, Inc.

Table of Contents

Introduction

MS-DOS Quick Reference is not a rehash of traditional documentation. Instead, this quick reference is a compilation of the most frequently-used information from Que's best-selling DOS books.

MS-DOS Quick Reference presents essential information on MS-DOS commands, batch files, error messages, and the elusive EDLIN commands. You'll learn the proper use of primary MS-DOS functions, as well as how to avoid serious errors. Thanks to the MS-DOS Survival Guide, you'll also learn the proper DOS commands to use for specific operations. In all, MS-DOS Quick Reference contains fundamental DOS information in a compact, easy-to-use format.

While MS-DOS Quick Reference contains essential DOS information, it is not intended as a replacement for the comprehensive information presented in a full-size handbook. You should supplement this quick reference with one of Que's complete DOS texts, such as *MS-DOS User's Guide*, 3rd Edition, *Using PC DOS*, 2nd Edition, or *Managing Your Hard Disk*, 2nd Edition.

Now you can put essential information at your fingertips with *MS-DOS Quick Reference*—and the entire *Que Quick Reference Series*!

MS-DOS Command Reference

The *Command Reference* includes all the MS-DOS commands. Each command is presented in the same format: the command name appears first, followed by the terms *Internal* or *External*. These indicate whether the command is built into MS-DOS (internal) or is disk-resident (external).

The command's purpose is explained, followed by the syntax required to invoke the command and the rules for its use. An example is given for some of the commands.

The "Notes" section contains additional comments, information, hints, or suggestions for using the command.

Notation

The notation used to represent a file specification is

    d:path**filename**.*ext*

d: is the name of the disk drive holding the file, and *path*\\ is the directory path to the file. **filename** is the root name of the file, and *.ext* is the file name extension.

If any part of this notation does not appear in the file specification (under "Syntax"), the omitted part is not allowed with this command. For example, the notation **d:filename.ext** indicates that path names are not allowed in the command.

In most cases, a device name may be substituted for a full file specification.

If a notation under "Syntax" appears in blue, the notation is mandatory and must be entered. If a notation appears in *italics*, the notation is optional and is entered only when appropriate.

Notation for External Commands and Batch Files

Starting with MS-DOS V3, external commands (which are simply program files) and batch files residing in different subdirectories can be executed just as program and batch files on different disks can be executed. The syntax used in this summary has a *c* added to the disk drive name and path. The notation is

dc:pathc\command_name

dc: is the name of the disk drive holding the command, *pathc*\ is the directory path to the command, and command_name is the name of the program or batch file to execute.

This notation is valid for external commands, those disk-resident commands that are not an internal part of COMMAND.COM, and for batch files.

In this command notation, the following rules apply:

1. If you do not give a disk drive name for the command (*dc:*), MS-DOS will search for the command on the current disk drive.

2. If you do not give a path (*pathc*\), MS-DOS will search for the command on the current directory of the current disk (or the current directory of the specified disk drive if one was given).

3. If you do not give a drive name and a path name, MS-DOS will search the current directory of the current disk for the command. If the command is not found, MS-DOS will search the list of paths specified by the PATH command. If MS-DOS does not find the command after searching the path, MS-DOS displays the error message

```
Bad command or file name
```

and gives the MS-DOS system prompt (usually A>
or C>).

Using Upper- and Lowercase Letters

Words appearing in uppercase letters under "Syntax" are
the words you must type. Words that appear in lowercase letters are variables. Be sure to substitute the
appropriate disk drive letter or name, path name, file
name, etc., for the lowercase variable when you type the
command.

Commands, as well as all parameters and switches typed
with commands, may be entered in either upper- or
lowercase. The exceptions are FIND and the batch
subcommands; for these commands, the use of upper- or
lowercase for certain parameters may be important.

APPEND

(Set directory search order)   *External*

Purpose

Instructs MS-DOS to search the specified directories on
the specified disks if a nonprogram/nonbatch file is not
found in the current directory

Syntax

To establish the data file search path the first time, use:

*dc:pathc***APPEND** *d1 :path1 ;d2 :path2 ;d3 :path3 ;. . .*

To use either of APPEND's switches, use:

*dc:pathc***APPEND** */X /E*

To change the data file search path, use:

*dc:pathc***APPEND** *d1 :path1 ;d2 :path2 ;d3 :path3 ;. . .*

To see the search path, use:

  *dc:pathc***APPEND**

To disconnect the data file search, use:

  *dc:pathc***APPEND;**

dc: is the name of the disk drive holding the command.

pathc is the path to the command.

d1:, *d2:*, and *d3:* are valid disk drive names.

path1, *path2*, and *path3* are valid path names to the
directories you want MS-DOS to search for
nonprogram/nonbatch files.

Switches
   /X Redirects programs that use the MS-DOS function
       calls SEARCH FIRST, FIND FIRST, and EXEC.

   /E Places the disk drive paths in the *environment*.

ASSIGN

(Assign disk drive)   *External*

Purpose

Instructs MS-DOS to use a disk drive other than the one
specified by a program or command

Syntax

To reroute drive activity, use

  *dc:pathc***ASSIGN d1=d2** . . .

dc: is the name of the disk drive holding the command.

pathc is the path to the command.

d1 is the letter of the disk drive the program or MS-DOS normally uses.

d2 is the letter of the disk drive that you want the program or DOS to use, instead of the usual drive.

The three periods (. . .) represent additional disk drive assignments.

To clear the reassignment, use:

    *dc:pathc***ASSIGN**

Examples

    a.   **ASSIGN A = C** or **ASSIGN A=C**

MS-DOS reroutes to drive C any activity for drive A. A space may appear on either side of the equal sign.

    b.   **ASSIGN A=C B=C**

MS-DOS reroutes to drive C any requests for activity for drives A and B.

    c.   **ASSIGN**

Any previous drive reassignment is cleared.

ATTRIB

(Change/show file attributes)   *External*

Purpose

Displays, sets, or clears a file's read-only or archive attributes

---
Syntax

To set the file's attributes on, use

    *dc:pathc***ATTRIB +R +A** *d:path***filename.ext**

To clear the file's attributes, use

   dc:pathc**ATTRIB -R -A** *d:path***filename.ext**

To display a file's read-only and archive status, use

   dc:pathc**ATTRIB** *d:path***filename.ext**

dc: is the name of the disk drive holding the command.

pathc\\ is the path to the command.

R is the read-only attribute.

A is the archive attribute (V3.2 and later).

+ turns on the attribute (the file becomes read-only or marked as created/changed).

- turns off the attribute (the file is writeable or marked as not created/changed).

d: is the name of the disk drive holding the files for which the read-only attribute will be displayed or changed.

path\\ is the path to the files for which the read-only attribute will be displayed or changed.

filename.ext is the name of the file for which the read-only attribute will be displayed or changed. Wild cards are permitted.

_____
Switch

   /S   Sets or clears the attributes of the specified files in the specified directory and all subdirectories to that directory.

BACKUP

(Back up diskettes or hard disks)   *External*

Purpose

Backs up one or more files from a hard disk or a diskette onto a diskette or another hard disk.

Syntax

*dc:pathc***BACKUP** **d1:***path\\filename.ext* **d2:**
/S /M /A /D:date /T:time /F /L:dl:filenamel:extl

dc: is the name of the disk drive holding the command.

pathc is the path to the command.

d1: is the name of the hard disk or floppy disk drive to be backed up.

path is the initial directory path for backup.

filename.ext is the name of the file(s) you want to back up. Wild cards are allowed.

d2: is the hard disk or floppy disk drive that will receive the backup files.

Examples

The following examples use a hierarchical directory set up on the hard disk (C:). The directory named WORD is a subdirectory of the root directory; the directory named LETTERS is a subdirectory of WORD. For each set of examples (lettered A through G), the current directory is indicated.

Example A. Current directory: root

(1) **BACKUP C: A:**
(2) **BACKUP C:*.* A:**

Both commands have the same effect. They back up the files only in the root directory.

Example B. Current directory: LETTERS

(1) **BACKUP C: A:**
(2) **BACKUP C:\WORDS\LETTERS A:**
(3) **BACKUP C:\WORDS\LETTERS*.* A:**
(4) **BACKUP . A:**

All four commands have the same effect. They back up all files in the directory LETTERS. Examples A-1 and B-1 tell MS-DOS to back up all the files in the current directory from drive C to drive A. These examples are based on the assumption that you are using the directory you want to back up. Because you have not given a file name, BACKUP "assumes" that all files should be backed up.

A backslash (\) at the beginning of a path name tells MS-DOS to start with the root directory of the disk. Because the root directory is the only specified directory on the path, only the root directory's contents are backed up. When a period (current directory symbol) is used as a path name, the effect is the same as giving no path.

Examples B-2 and B-3 both back up all files in the LETTERS subdirectory on the disk. The directory to be used for the backup is the last named directory in the chain, or path. BACKUP assumes that you mean all files if no file name is given.

Example C. Current directory: LETTERS

(1) **BACKUP C:*.LET A:**
(2) **BACKUP C:\WORDS\LETTERS*.LET A:**

Examples C-1 and C-2 back up all files with the file name extension .LET in the directory LETTERS. The difference between C-1 and C-2 is that C-2 can be issued while you are using a directory other than LETTERS. For you to use C-1, however, the current directory must be LETTERS.

Example D. Current directory: root

(1) BACKUP C: A: /S

The /S switch tells MS-DOS to start with the directory indicated and move down through all the subdirectories.

Example E. Current directory: root

(1) BACKUP C:\ A: /S /D:8/21/88
(2) BACKUP C:\ A: /S /D:08-21-88

In both lines, BACKUP backs up in every directory on drive C all files created or changed since August 21, 1988. Slashes or hyphens are acceptable between the numbers, and leading zeros are not necessary with one-digit months or days. You can omit spaces between the starting slash of the switch and the ending number in the date.

Example F. Current directory: root

BACKUP C:\ A: /S /D:08-21-88 /A

Like F-1, this command backs up all hard disk files created or changed since the given date. The difference is that the /A switch directs BACKUP to add these files to the backup diskette without deleting the old files. Without the /A switch, any files in the \BACKUP subdirectory (if you are backing up onto another hard disk) or on the backup diskette will be erased.

Example G. Current directory: root

BACKUP C:\ A: /S /M

The /M switch tells BACKUP to back up any files that do not have the archive bit set. An archive bit is a special area kept in the directory for each file. When you create or modify a file, the archive bit is turned off. When you back up a file, the archive bit is turned on.

When you use the /M switch, BACKUP skips any file
whose archive bit is turned on. This means that
BACKUP will back up any file or version of a file you
have not backed up before.

BREAK

(Ctrl-Break Checking)   *Internal*

Purpose

Determines when MS-DOS looks for a Ctrl-Break or
Ctrl-C to stop a program

Syntax

To turn on BREAK, use:

   BREAK ON

To turn off BREAK, use:

   BREAK OFF

To find out whether BREAK is on or off, use:

   BREAK

CHCP

(Change code page)   *Internal*

Purpose

For as many devices as possible, changes the code page
(font) used by MS-DOS

Syntax

To change the current code page, use:

   CHCP codepage

To display the current code page, use:

CHCP

codepage is a valid three-digit code page number.

CHDIR or CD

(Change directory)   *Internal*

Purpose

Changes the current directory or shows the path of the current directory

Syntax

To change the current directory, use:

CHDIR *d:*path

or

CD *d:*path

To show the current directory path on a disk drive, use:

CHDIR *d:*

or

CD *d:*

d: is a valid disk drive name.

path is a valid directory path.

Rules

1. If you do not indicate a disk drive, the current disk drive is used.

2. When you give a path name, MS-DOS moves from

the current directory to the last directory specified in the **path**.

3. If you want to start the move with the disk's root directory, use the backslash (\) as the path's first character. Otherwise, MS-DOS assumes that the path starts with the current directory.

4. If you give an invalid **path**, MS-DOS displays an error message and remains in the current directory.

Examples
Example A. Starting from the root directory:

CHDIR DOS

MS-DOS moves from the root directory to the directory named DOS.

Example B. Starting from the root directory:

CHDIR DOS\HARDDISK

MS-DOS moves from the root directory to HARDDISK.

Example C. Starting from the \DOS\HARDDISK directory:

(1) **CHDIR ..**
(2) **CHDIR \DOS**

MS-DOS moves from HARDDISK back to the DOS directory.

These two examples illustrate different ways to move between directories. **CHDIR ..** shows how to move up to a parent directory. MS-DOS does not permit movement by parent directory name when you are working in a subdirectory. Therefore, you cannot move up a level from HARDDISK to DOS by typing the line

CHDIR DOS. If you give this command, MS-DOS "thinks" you are trying to move to a HARDDISK subdirectory named DOS instead of trying to move up a level. The only way you can move up one level is by using the parent directory symbol (..).

CHDIR \DOS shows how to move from the disk's root directory to the correct directory. Notice that the first character in the directory name is the path character, the backslash (\). When you use the backslash as a path name's first character, MS-DOS returns to the root directory and then moves down one level to the DOS directory.

CHKDSK

(Check disk)   *External*

Purpose

Checks the directory and the file allocation table (FAT) of the disk and reports disk and memory status. CHKDSK can also repair errors in the directories or the FAT.

Syntax

        *dc:pathc***CHKDSK** *d:path\filename.ext/F/V*

dc: is the name of the disk drive holding the command.

pathc is the path to the command.

d: is the name of the disk drive to be analyzed.

path is the directory path to the files to be analyzed.

filename.ext is a valid MS-DOS file name. Wild cards are permitted.

Switches

     /F   Fixes the file allocation table and other problems

/V Shows CHKDSK's progress and displays more
detailed information about the errors the program
finds. (This switch is known as the verbose switch.)

Examples

1. **CHKDSK**

MS-DOS analyzes the disk or diskette in the current
drive.

2. **CHKDSK B:**

MS-DOS analyzes the diskette in drive B.

3. **CHKDSK A: /F**

MS-DOS analyzes the diskette in drive A and asks
permission to repair the file allocation table (FAT) if a
flaw is found. In case of a flaw, one message may be

```
xxxx lost clusters found in xxx chains
Convert lost chains to files (Y/N)?_
```

If you answer **Y** for yes, CHKDSK converts into files
the lost areas of the disk. These files will appear in the
root directory of the disk and use the name
FILExxxx .CHK, in which xxxx is a consecutive
number between 0000 and 9999. If these files do not
contain anything useful, you can delete them.

4. **CHKDSK /V**

MS-DOS invokes the verbose mode, which lists each
directory and subdirectory on the disk and all files in the
directories. This output can be redirected to a file or
printer.

5. **CHKDSK *.***

MS-DOS checks all files in the current directory on the
current drive to see whether they are stored contiguously
on the disk. Two messages may be displayed:

```
All  specified  file(s)  are  contiguous
```

This message means that you are getting good disk
performance.

```
d:path\filename.ext
Contains  xxx  noncontiguous  blocks
```

When this message appears, the specified files are not
stored contiguously on the disk. The message is
displayed for each file not stored contiguously. If you
are analyzing a diskette and many file names are listed,
you will probably want to COPY (not DISKCOPY) the
files to another diskette. In the case of the hard disk,
BACKUP your entire hard disk, reformat it, and
RESTORE it.

CLS

(Clear screen)   *Internal*

Purpose

Erases the display screen

Syntax

CLS

Rules

1. All information on the screen is cleared, and the
   cursor is placed at the home position (upper left
   corner).

2. This command affects only the active video display.

3. If you have used the ANSI control codes to set the
   foreground and background, the color settings
   remain in effect.

4. If you have not set the foreground/background color, the screen reverts to light characters on a dark background.

5. CLS affects only the screen, not memory.

COMMAND

(Invoke secondary command processor)
External

Purpose

Invokes a second copy of COMMAND.COM, the command processor

Syntax

*dc:pathc***COMMAND** */E:size /P /C string*

dc: is the name of the drive where MS-DOS can find a copy of COMMAND.COM.

pathc is the MS-DOS path to the copy of COMMAND.COM.

string is the set of characters you pass to the new copy of the command interpreter.

Switches

/E:size   Sets the *size* of the *environment*. Size is a decimal number from 160 to 32,768 bytes, rounded up to the nearest multiple of 16.

/P   Keeps this copy permanently in memory (until the next system reset).

/C   Passes the string of commands (the string) to the new copy of COMMAND.COM.

COMP

(Compare files)   *External*

Purpose

Compares two sets of disk files to see whether they are the same or different

Syntax

> *dc:pathc***COMP** *d1:path1\\filename1.ext1*
> *d2:path2\\filename2.ext2*

dc: is the name of the disk drive holding the command.

pathc is the path to the command.

d1: is the drive containing the first set of files to be compared.

path1 is the path to the first set of files.

filename1.ext1 is the file name for the first set of files. Wild cards are allowed.

d2: is the drive containing the second set of files to be compared.

path2 is the path to the second set of files.

filename2.ext2 is the file name for the second set of files. Wild cards are allowed.

d1 and *d2* may be the same.

path1 and *path2* may be the same.

filename1.ext1 and *filename2.ext2* may be the same also.

Terms

d1:path1\\filename1.ext1 is the *primary* file set.

d2:path2\\filename2.ext2 is the *secondary* file set.

Rules

1. If you do not give a drive name for a set, the current disk drive is used. (This rule applies to *d1:* and *d2:*, as well as to *dc:*, the drive holding the command itself.)

2. If you do not give a path for a file set, the current directory for the drive is used.

3. If you do not enter a file name for a file set, all files for that set (primary or secondary) are compared (which is the same as entering *.*). However, only the files in the secondary set with names matching file names in the primary set are compared.

4. If you do not enter a drive name, path name, and file name, COMP prompts you for the primary and secondary file sets to compare. Otherwise, the correct diskettes must be in the correct drive if you are comparing files on diskettes. COMP does not wait for you to insert diskettes if you give both primary and secondary file names.

5. Only normal disk files are checked. Hidden or system files and directories are not checked.

6. Files with matching names but different lengths are not checked. A message is printed indicating that these files are different.

7. After ten mismatches (unequal comparisons) between the contents of two compared files, COMP automatically ends the comparison between the two files and aborts.

Example

    COMP A:FRED.LET C:FRED.LET

The file in the current directory on drive A, FRED.LET, is compared to the file in the current directory on drive C, FRED.LET.

Notes

If you have a program that once functioned properly but is now acting strangely, check a good backup copy of the file against the copy you are using. If COMP finds differences, copy the good program to the disk you are using.

Do not compare files you are using now with copies that have been archived by the BACKUP program. If your only backup copy of a program is in a backed-up file, use RESTORE to place the file in a directory, and then COMPare the files.

When you are trying to find the last revision of a file, look at its date and time in the directory to identify the most recent revision of a file. If you want to compare diskettes that have been copied with DISKCOPY, use DISKCOMP instead of COMP.

Configuration Subcommand

BREAK (Ctrl-Break Checking)   *Internal*

Purpose

Determines when MS-DOS looks for a Ctrl-Break or Ctrl-C to stop a program

Syntax

To turn on BREAK, use:

   BREAK = ON

To turn off BREAK, use:

   BREAK = OFF

Configuration Subcommand

BUFFERS (Set number of disk buffers)   Internal

Purpose

Sets the number of disk buffers set aside by MS-DOS in memory

Syntax

BUFFERS = nn

nn is the number of buffers to set, in the range of 1 to 99.

Configuration Subcommand

COUNTRY (Set country-dependent information)
Internal

Purpose

Instructs MS-DOS to modify the input and display of date, time, and field divider information

Syntax

COUNTRY = nnn

nnn is the country code.

Configuration Subcommand

DEVICE (Set device driver)   Internal

Purpose

Instructs MS-DOS to load, link, and use a special device driver

Syntax

DEVICE = d:path\filename.ext

d: is the name of the drive where MS-DOS can find the device drive to be used.

path is the MS-DOS path to the device driver.

filename.*ext* is the root file name and optional extension of the device driver.

Configuration Subcommand

FCBS (set control blocks) *Internal*

Purpose

Specifies the number of MS-DOS File Control Blocks that can be open simultaneously, and how many to keep open all the time

Syntax

FCBS = maxopen,*neverclose*

maxopen is the number of FCBs that can be open at any given time.

neverclose is the number of FCBs that are always open.

Configuration Subcommand

FILES (set maximum open files) *Internal*

Purpose

Specifies the number of file handles that may be open at any given time

Syntax

FILES = nnn

nnn is the number of file handles that may be open at any given time.

Configuration Subcommand

LASTDRIVE (specify last system drive)   Internal

Purpose

Sets the last valid drive letter acceptable to MS-DOS

Syntax

LASTDRIVE = x

x is the alphabetical character for the highest system drive.

Configuration Subcommand

SHELL (specify command processor)   Internal

Purpose

Changes the default MS-DOS command processor

Syntax

SHELL = *d:path*filename.*ext*

d: is the name of the drive where MS-DOS can find the command processor to be used.

path is the MS-DOS path to the command processor.

filename.*ext* is the root file name and optional extension of the command processor.

COPY

(Copy files)   *Internal*

Purpose

Copies files between disk drives and/or devices, either keeping the same file name or changing it. COPY can concatenate (join) two or more files into another file or append one or more files to another file. Options support

special handling of text files and verification of the
copying process.

Syntax

To copy a file, use:

COPY /A/B d1:path1\filename1.ext1 /A/B
d0:path2/filename0.ext0 /A/B/V

or

COPY /A/B d1:path1\filename1.ext1 /A/B/V

To join several files into one file, use:

COPY /A/B d1:path1\filename1.ext1 /A/B
+ d2:path2\filename2.ext2 /A/B +...

d1:, d2:, and d0: are valid disk drive names.

path1\, path2\, and path0\ are valid path names.

filename1.ext1, filename2.ext2, and filename0.ext0 are
valid file names. Wild cards are allowed.

The three periods (...) represent additional files in the
form dx:pathx/filenamex.extx.

Terms

The file that is being copied from is the *source file*. The
names containing 1 and 2 are the source files.

The file that is being copied to is the *destination file*. It
is represented by a 0.

Switches

/V Verifies that the copy has been recorded correctly.
    The following switches have different effects for
    the source and the destination.

For the source file:

/A   Treats the file as an ASCII (text) file. The command copies all the information in the file up to, but not including, the end-of-file marker (Ctrl-Z). Anything after the end-of-file marker is ignored.

/B   Copies the entire file as if it were a program file (*binary1*). Any end-of-file markers (Ctrl-Z) are treated as normal characters, and the EOF characters are copied.

For the destination file:

/A   Adds an end-of-file marker (Ctrl-Z) to the end of the ASCII text file after it is copied.

/B   Does not add the end-of-file marker to this binary file.

CTTY

(Change console)   *Internal*

Purpose

Changes the standard input and output device to an auxiliary console, or changes the input and output device back from an auxiliary console to the keyboard and video display.

Syntax

CTTY device

device is the name of the device you want to use as the new standard input and output device. This name must be a valid MS- DOS device name.

Rules

1. The **device** should be a character-oriented device capable of both input and output.

2. Using a colon (:) after the device name is optional.

3. Programs designed to work with the video display's control codes may not function properly when redirected.

4. CTTY does not affect any other form of redirected I/O or piping. For example, the < (redirect from), the > (redirect to), and the | (pipe between programs) work as usual.

Examples

1. **CTTY COM1**

This command makes the device attached to COM1 the new console. The peripheral connected to COM1 must be a terminal or a teleprinter (printer with a keyboard). After you give this command, MS-DOS expects normal input to come from COM1 and sends anything for the video display to COM1.

2. **CTTY CON:**

This command makes the keyboard and video display the console. In effect, this command cancels the first example. The colon after CON or any other valid MS-DOS device name is optional.

Notes

The CTTY command was designed so that a terminal or teleprinter, instead of the computer's keyboard and video display, can be used for console input and output. This added versatility has little effect on most users.

You must specify a device that can both receive input and send output to the computer system. Using CTTY with a normal printer (an output-only device) is a mistake. MS-DOS will patiently wait forever for you to type commands on the printer's nonexistent keyboard.

DATE

(Set/show date)   *Internal*

Purpose

Displays and/or changes the system date

Syntax

DATE *date_string*

date_string is in one of the following forms:

mm-dd-yy or *mm-dd-yyyy* for North America
dd-mm-yy or *dd-mm-yyyy* for Europe
yy-mm-dd or *yyyy-mm-dd* for the Far East

mm is a one- or two-digit number for the month (1 to 12).

dd is a one- or two-digit number for the day (1 to 31).

yy is a one- or two-digit number for the year (80 to 99). The 19 is assumed.

yyyy is a four-digit number for the year (1980 to 2099).

The delimiters between the day, month, and year can be hyphens, periods, or slashes. The result displayed will vary, depending on the country code set in the CONFIG.SYS file.

DEL

(Delete files)   *Internal*

Purpose

Deletes files from the disk

DEL is an alternative command for ERASE, and performs the same functions. See ERASE for a complete description.

DIR

(Directory)   *Internal*

Purpose

Lists any or all files and subdirectories in a disk's directory

The DIR command displays the following:

Disk volume name (if any)
Name of the directory (its complete path)
Name of each disk file or subdirectory
Number of files
Amount, in bytes, of free space on the disk

The DIR command, unless otherwise directed, shows also the following:

Number of bytes occupied by each file
Date/time of the file's creation/last update

Syntax

DIR *d:path\filename.ext* /P/W

d: is the drive holding the disk you want to examine.

path is the path to the directory you want to examine.

filename.ext is a valid file name. Wild cards are permitted.

Switches

/P Pauses when the screen is full and waits for you to press any key.

/W Gives a wide (80-column) display of the names of the files. The information about file size, date, and time is not displayed.

Notes

The DIR command finds the disk files or subdirectories on the disk. This command shows only the files and subdirectories in the specified (or default) directory. To see a list of all the files on a disk, use **CHKDSK** /**V** or **TREE** /**F**.

You can print the directory by typing **DIR >PRN**, or you can put a copy of the directory into a file by typing **DIR > filename1**. Here, **filename1** is the name of the file to hold the directory.

═ DISKCOMP ════════════

(Compare diskettes)   *External*

Purpose

Compares two diskettes on a track-for-track, sector-for-sector basis to see whether their contents are identical

Syntax

*dc:pathc***DISKCOMP** *d1: d2: /1 /8*

dc: is the name of the disk drive holding the command.

pathc is the path to the command.

d1: and *d2:* are the disk drives that hold the diskettes to be compared. These drives may be the same or different drives.

Switches

/*1* Compares only the first side of the diskette, even if the diskette or disk drive is double-sided.

/*8* Compares only 8 sectors per track, even if the first diskette has a different number of sectors per track.

Rules

1. If you do not give a drive name, the first floppy disk drive (usually drive A) is used.

2. If you give only one valid floppy disk drive name, it is used for the comparison.

3. Giving the same valid floppy disk drive name twice is the same as giving only one disk drive name.

4. If you give a valid hard disk drive name or invalid disk drive name, MS-DOS displays an error message and does not perform the comparison.

5. When you are using one disk drive (rules 1-4), MS- DOS prompts you to change diskettes.

6. Only compatible diskettes should be compared. The two diskettes must be formatted with the same number of tracks, sectors, and sides.

7. Do not use DISKCOMP with an ASSIGNed disk drive. DISKCOMP ignores the effects of the ASSIGN.

8. Do not use a JOINed disk, a SUBSTituted disk, a virtual (RAM) disk, or networked disk drives with DISKCOMP. MS-DOS displays an error message if you do.

Example

DISKCOMP A: B:

MS-DOS compares the diskette in drive A with the diskette in drive B.

DISKCOPY

(Copy entire diskette)   *External*

Purpose

Copies the entire contents of one diskette to another
diskette on a track-for-track basis (making a "carbon
copy"). DISKCOPY works only with diskettes.

Syntax

>   *dc:pathc***DISKCOPY** *d1: d2: /1*

dc: is the name of the disk drive holding the command.

pathc is the path to the command.

d1: is the floppy disk drive that holds the source
(original) diskette.

d2: is the floppy disk drive that holds the target diskette
(diskette to be copied to).

Switch

/1 Copies only the first side of the diskette.

Terms

The diskette you are copying from is the *source* or *first*
diskette.

The diskette you are copying to is the *target* or *second*
diskette.

ERASE

(Erase files)   *Internal*

Purpose

Removes one or more files from the directory

Syntax

>   **ERASE** *d:path\\filename.ext*

or

DEL *d:path\filename.ext*

d: is the name of the disk drive holding the file(s) to be erased.

path is the directory of the file(s) to be erased.

filename.ext is the name of the file(s) to be erased. Wild cards are allowed.

EXE2BIN

(Change .EXE files into .BIN or .COM files)
                                              External

Purpose

Changes suitably formatted .EXE files into .BIN or .COM files

Syntax

*dc:pathc***EXE2BIN** *d1:path1/***filename1***.ext1*
    d2:path2/filename2.ext2

dc: is the name of the disk drive holding the command.

pathc is the path to the command.

d1: is the name of the disk drive holding the file to be converted.

path1/ is the directory of the file to be converted.

filename1 is the root name of the file to be converted.

.ext1 is the extension name of the file to be converted.

d2: is the name of the disk drive for the output file.

path2/ is the directory of the output file.

filename2 is the root name of the output file.

.ext2 is the extension name of the output file.

Terms

The file to be converted is the *source* file.

The output file is the *destination* file.

Rules

1. If you do not specify a drive for the source file, the current drive is used as the source file.

2. If you do not specify a drive for the destination file, the source drive is used.

3. When you do not specify a path, the current directory of the disk is used.

4. You must specify a root name for the source file (the file to be converted).

5. If you do not specify a root name for the destination file, the root name of the source file is used.

6. If you do not specify an extension for the source file, the extension .EXE is used.

7. If you do not specify an extension for the destination file, the extension .BIN is used.

8. The .EXE file must be in the correct format (following Microsoft conventions).

Notes

EXE2BIN is a programming utility that converts .EXE (executable) program files to .COM or .BIN (binary image) files. The resulting program takes less disk space and loads faster. This conversion, however, may be a disadvantage in future versions of MS-DOS. Unless you are using a compiler-based language, you will probably

never use this command. For further information on
EXE2BIN, see your MS-DOS manual.

EXIT

(Leave secondary command processor)   *Internal*

Purpose

Leaves a secondary command processor and return to
the primary

Syntax

EXIT

Rules

This command has no effect if a secondary command
processor is not loaded or if it was loaded with the */P*
switch.

FASTOPEN

(Fast opening of files)   *External*

Purpose

Keeps directory information in memory so that
MS-DOS can quickly find and use files you
frequently need

Syntax

*dc:pathc***FASTOPEN d:**=*nnn . . .*

dc: is the name of the disk drive holding the command.

pathc is the path to the command.

d: is the name of the disk drive whose directory
information should be held in memory.
nnn is the number of directory entries to be held in
memory (10 to 999).

. . . designates additional disk drives in the form
d:=*nnn*.

FIND

(Find string filter)   *External*

Purpose

Displays from the designated files all the lines that
match (or do not match) the specified string. This
command can also display the line numbers.

Syntax

dc:pathc**FIND** */V/C/N* "**string**" *d:path\filename.ext...*

dc: is the name of the disk drive holding the command.

pathc is the path to the command.

string is the set of characters for which you want to
search. As indicated, **string** must be enclosed in
quotation marks.

d: is the name of the disk drive for the file.

path is the directory holding the file.

filename.ext is name of the file you want to search.

Switches

/V Displays all lines that do not contain **string**.

/C Counts the number of times that **string** occurs in
the file but does not display the lines.

/N Displays the line number (number of the line in the
file) before each line that contains **string**.

=FORMAT

(Format disk)   ***External***

Purpose

Initializes a disk to accept MS-DOS information and files. FORMAT also checks the disk for defective tracks and (optionally) places MS-DOS on the diskette or hard disk.

Syntax

*dc:pathc***FORMAT** *d: /S/1/8/V/B/4/N:ss/T:tt*

dc: is the name of the disk drive holding the command.

pathc is the path to the command.

d: is a valid disk drive name.

Switches

/S	Places a copy of the operating system on the disk so that it is bootable
/1	Formats only the first side of the diskette
/8	Formats an 8-sector diskette (V1)
/B	Formats an 8-sector diskette and leaves the proper places in the directory for any version of the operating system but does not place the operating system on the diskette
/4	Formats a diskette in a high-capacity disk drive for double-sided (320K/360K) use
/N:ss	Formats the disk with *ss* number of sectors, ranging from 1 to 99
/T:tt	Formats the disk with *ttt* number of tracks per side, ranging from 1 to 999

Rules

1. If you do not give a disk drive name, the current disk drive is used.

2. Before you can use a new diskette, it must be formatted. The only exception occurs when you use a new diskette as the target for DISKCOPY or BACKUP (with the /F switch).

3. MS-DOS checks the floppy disk drive. Unless otherwise directed through a switch, MS-DOS formats the diskette to its maximum capacity: 2 sides if a double-sided drive is used; 9 sectors per track for normal disk drives, and 15 sectors per track for HC disk drives.

4. Some switches do not work together. For example, you cannot use the following switch combinations:

   a. /V or /S with /B

   b. /V with /8

   c. /N or /T with a 320/360K or hard disk drive

   d. /1, /4, /8, or /B with a hard disk

5. Format destroys any information previously recorded on the disk. Do not FORMAT a disk that contains any useful information.

6. To make a diskette usable with all versions of MS- DOS, use the /B and /1 switches. (Format the diskette for any MS-DOS version and format only one side.)

7. If you give a volume name, it can be 1 to 11 characters long and contain any character that is legal in a file name.

8. If you use the /S switch (to place the operating system on a disk) and the current directory does not have a copy of MS-DOS, MS-DOS prompts you to put the MS-DOS diskette into drive A so that the system gets the copy of MS-DOS before formatting the disk.

9. If MS-DOS formats a hard disk that has a volume label, it asks

```
Enter current Volume Label for drive d:
```

To continue formatting disk drive d, enter the disk drive's current volume label. If you do not enter the exact volume label, FORMAT displays

```
Invalid Volume ID
Format Failure
```

and aborts.

10. If you are formatting a hard disk without a volume label, FORMAT displays the message:

```
WARNING, ALL DATA ON NON-REMOVABLE
   DISK DRIVE d: WILL BE LOST!
Proceed with Format (Y/N?)
```

Answer Y for Yes to format the hard disk drive d, N for No to abort FORMAT from formatting the hard disk.

11. Although the /4 switch may be used to create double-sided diskettes in a high-capacity disk drive, the formatted diskette is not reliable when used in double-sided disk drives.

12. You cannot format a RAM disk (VDISK), a networked disk, a diskette on an ASSIGNed disk drive, a SUBSTituted disk drive, or a JOINed disk drive.

GRAFTABL

(Load graphics table)   *External*

Purpose

Loads into memory the tables of additional character sets to be displayed on the Color/Graphics Adapter (CGA)

Syntax

To install or change the table used by the CGA, use:

  *dc:pathc***GRAFTABL** *codepage*

To display the number of the current table, use:

  *dc:pathc***GRAFTABL** /**STATUS**

To show the options available for use with GRAFTABL, use:

  *dc:pathc***GRAFTABL** ?

dc: is the name of the disk drive holding the command.

pathc is the path to the command.

codepage is the three-digit number of the code page for the display.

GRAPHICS

(Graphics screen print)   *External*

Purpose

Prints the graphics screen contents on a suitable printer

Syntax

  *dc:pathc***GRAPHICS** *printer* /*R* /*B*

dc: is the name of the disk drive holding the command.

pathc is the path to the command.

printer is the type of printer you are using. The printer may be one of the following:

COLOR1 — Color Printer with a black ribbon

COLOR4 — Color Printer with an RGB (red, green, blue, and black) ribbon, producing four colors

COLOR8 — Color Printer with a CMY (cyan, magenta, yellow, and black) ribbon, producing eight colors

GRAPHICS — Graphics Printer

Switches

/R *Reverses* print colors so that the image on the paper matches the screen (that is, produces a white-on-black image)

/B Prints the *background* color of the screen. You can use this switch only when printer type is COLOR4 or COLOR8.

Rules

1. If you use this command to print the graphics screen contents, your printer must be compatible with the IBM Color Printer or Graphics Matrix Printer.

2. If you do not specify a *printer*, a Graphics Matrix Printer is assumed.

3. If you do not use the /R (reverse) switch, an inverse image is printed, black on white. White images on the screen are printed as dark colors, and black images are printed as white images.

4. If you do not use the /B switch, the background

color of the screen is not printed. The /B switch has
no effect unless you specify the printer type
COLOR4 or COLOR8.

5. When you choose the 320-by-200 (medium-
resolution) mode, the printer prints in four shades of
gray, corresponding to the four possible colors.
When you specify the 640-by-200 (high-
resolution) mode, the printer prints in black and
white, but the printout is rotated 90 degrees to the
left. (The upper right corner of the screen is placed
on the upper left corner of the printout.)

6. The only way to deactivate GRAPHICS is to reset
your computer.

Notes

The names COLOR4 and COLOR8 are logical on the
Color Printer. The red-green-blue-black ribbon produces
four colors (five if you include the color of the paper
itself). The cyan-magenta-yellow-black ribbon produces
eight colors through combinations of overstriking one
color on another. For the video display, the primary
colors are red, green, and blue. For printing, the primary
colors are cyan, magenta, and yellow.

JOIN

(Join disk drives)   *External*

Purpose

Produces a single directory structure by connecting a
disk drive to a subdirectory of a second disk drive

Syntax

To connect disk drives, use:

*dc:pathc***JOIN d1:** *d2:***directoryname**

To disconnect disk drives, use:

*dc:pathc***JOIN d1: /D**

To show currently connected drives, use:

*dc:pathc***JOIN**

dc: is the name of the disk drive holding the command.

pathc is the path to the command.

d1: is the name of the disk drive to be connected.

d2: is the name of the disk drive to which **d1:** is connected.

\\directoryname is the name of a subdirectory in the root directory of d2 (the host). **\\directoryname** holds the connection to **d1** (the guest).

_____

Switch

/D Disconnects the specified guest disk drive from its host.

_____

Terms

The disk drive being connected is called the *guest disk drive*.

The disk drive and the subdirectory to which the guest disk drive is connected are the *host disk drive* and the *host subdirectory*.

KEYB

(Enable foreign language keys)   *External*

Purpose

Changes the keyboard layout and characters to one of five non-American-English languages

Syntax

To change the current keyboard layout, use:

> *dc:pathc:***KEYB** *keycode, codepage,*
>   *d:path\\KEYBOARD.SYS*

To display the current values for KEYB, use:

> *dc:pathc:***KEYB**

dc: is the name of the disk drive holding the command.

pathc is the path to the command.

keycode is the two-character keyboard code for your location. For MS-DOS V3.3 only five languages are available:

FR	France
GR	Germany
IT	Italy
SP	Spain
UK	United Kingdom

LABEL

(Volume label)   *External*

Purpose

Creates, changes, or deletes a volume label for a disk

Syntax

> *dc:pathc***LABEL** *d:volume_label*

dc: is the name of the disk drive holding the command.

pathc is the path to the command.

d: is the name of the disk drive for which the label will be changed.

volume_label is the new volume label for the disk.

MKDIR or MD

(Make directory)   *Internal*

Purpose

Creates a subdirectory

Syntax

MKDIR *d:path*\dirname

or

MD *d:pat*h\dirname

d: is the name of the disk drive for the subdirectory.

path\ is a valid path name for the path to the directory that will hold the subdirectory.

dirname is the name of the subdirectory you are creating.

MODE

Purpose

Sets the mode of operation for the printer(s), the video display, and the Asynchronous Communications Adapter. Also controls code page switching for the console and printer.

MODE sets and controls the following: (1) the printer characteristics, (2) the characteristics of the video display and the display to use (when more than one display is in a system), (3) the characteristics of the Asynchronous Communications Adapter, (4) the redirection of printing between the parallel and serial printers, and (5) control of code pages.

Syntax

*dc:pathc***MODE LPT#:** *cpl, lpi, P*

or

*dc:pathc***MODE dt**

or

*dc:pathc***MODE** *dt,* s, *T*

or

*dc:pathc***MODE COMn: baud,** *parity, databits, stopbits, P*

or

*dc:pathc***MODE LPT#: = COMn**

or

*dc:pathc***MODE device CODEPAGE PREPARE =** ((**codepage,** *codepage, . . .*) *dp:pathp***pagefile.***ext*)

or

*dc:pathc***MODE device CODEPAGE SELECT = codepage**

or

*dc:pathc***MODE device CODEPAGE REFRESH**

or

*dc:pathc***MODE device CODEPAGE /*STATUS***

Where

dc: is the name of the disk drive holding the command.

pathc is the path to the command.

#: is the printer number (1, 2, or 3). The colon is optional.

cpl is the characters per line (80 or 132).

lpi is the lines per inch (6 or 8).

P specifies continuous retries on timeout errors.

dt is the display type, which may be one of the following values:

40 Sets the display to 40 characters per line for the graphics display

80 Sets the display to 80 characters per line for the graphics display

BW40 Makes the graphics display the active display and sets the mode to 40 characters per line, black and white (color disabled)

BW80 Makes the graphics display the active display and sets the mode to 80 characters per line, black and white (color disabled)

CO40 Makes the graphics display the active display and sets the mode to 40 characters per line (color disabled)

CO80 Makes the graphics display the active display and sets the mode to 80 characters per line (color disabled)

MONO Makes the Monochrome Display the active display

s shifts the graphics display right or left one character

T requests alignment of the graphics display screen with a one-line test pattern.

n: is the adapter number (1 or 2). The colon after the number is optional.

baud is the baud rate (110, 150, 300, 1200, 2400, 4800, or 9600).

parity is the parity checking (None, Odd, or Even).

databits is the number of data bits (7 or 8).

stopbits is the number of stop bits (1 or 2).

P represents continuous retries on timeout errors.

#: is the parallel printer number (1, 2, or 3). The colon is optional.

n is the Asynchronous Communications Adapter number (1 or 2).

device is the name of the device for which code page(s) will be chosen. Valid devices include:

CON:	The console
PRN:	The first parallel printer
LPT#:	Any parallel printer (# is 1, 2, or 3)

codepage is the number of the code page(s) to be used with the device. The number(s) must be:

437	United States
850	Multilingual
860	Portugal
863	French Canadian
865	Denmark/Norway

. . . represents additional code pages

dp: is the name of the disk drive holding the code page (font) information.

pathp is the path to the file holding the code page (font) information.

pagefile.*ext* is the name of the file holding the code page (font) information. Currently, the provided code page files are:

4201.CPI	IBM Proprinter
5202.CPI	IBM Quietwriter III printer
EGA.CPI	EGA type displays

Switch

/STATUS	displays the *status* of the device's code pages

MORE

(More output filter)   *External*

Purpose

Displays one screen of information from the standard input device and pauses while displaying the message — More —.   When you press any key, MORE displays the next screen of information.

Syntax

   *dc:pathc***MORE**

dc: is the name of the disk drive holding the command.

pathc is the path to the command.

Examples

   1. **MORE <TEST.TXT**

MORE dislays a screenful of information from the file TEST.TXT. MORE then displays the prompt

— More — at the bottom of the screen and waits for a keystroke. When you press a key, MORE continues this process until all information has been displayed. The command does not display the prompt on the final screenful of information.

2. **DIR | SORT | MORE**

MORE displays, 23 lines at a time, the sorted output of the directory command.

NLSFUNC

(National language support)   *External*

Purpose

Provides support for extended country information in MS-DOS and allows use of the CHCP command

Syntax

*dc:pathc*NLSFUNC *d:path*filename.*ext*

dc: is the name of the disk drive holding the command.

pathc is the path to the command.

d: is the name of the disk drive holding the country information file.

path is the path to the country information file.

filename.*ext* is the name of the file holding the country information. In MS-DOS V3.3, this information is contained in the file COUNTRY.SYS.

=| PATH |=

(Set directory search order)   *Internal*

Purpose

Tells MS-DOS to search the specified directories on the specified drives if a program or batch file is not found in the current directory

Syntax

PATH *d1:path1;d2:path2;d3:path3;...*

d1:, *d2:*, and *d3:* are valid disk drives names.

path1, *path2*, and *path3* are valid path names to the commands you want to run while in any directory.

The ellipsis (...) represents additional disk drives and path names.

=| PRINT |=

(Background printing)   *External*

Purpose

Prints a list of files on the printer while the computer performs other tasks

Syntax

*dc:pathc***PRINT** */D:device /B:bufsiz /M:maxtick*
  /Q:maxfiles /S:timeslice /U:busytick
  d1:path1\filename1.ext1 /P/T/C
  d2:path2\filename2.ext2 /P/T/C...

dc: is the name of the disk drive holding the command.

pathc is the path to the command.

d1: and *d2:* are valid disk drive names.

path1 and *path2* are valid path names to the files for printing.

filename1.ext1 and *filename2.ext2* are the names of the files you want to print. Wild cards are allowed.

The ellipsis (. . .) represents additional file names in the form of *dx:pathx\filenamex.extx* and are valid file specifications.

Switches

Switches Used When PRINT Is First Issued:

/B:bufsize	The size of the *buffer*
/D:device	The *device* to use
/M:maxtick	The *maximum* number of clock ticks to use
/Q:maxfiles	The maximum number of files to *queue*
/U:busytick	The number of clock ticks to wait for the printer
/S:timeslice	The number of times per *second* that PRINT can print (number of *timeslices*)

Switches Used Any Time You Issue PRINT:

/T	*Terminates* printing
/C	*Cancels* the printing of the file
/P	*Prints* this file

PROMPT

(Set the System Prompt) **Internal**

Purpose

Customizes the MS-DOS system prompt (the A>, or A prompt)

Syntax

PROMPT *promptstring*

promptstring is the text to be used for the new system prompt.

Rules

1. If you do not enter the promptstring, the standard system prompt reappears (A>).

2. Any text entered for *promptstring* becomes the new system prompt. You may enter special characters with the meta-strings.

3. The new system prompt stays in effect until you restart MS-DOS or reissue the PROMPT command.

4. To see the text of PROMPT after it has been set, use the SET command.

5. To start the prompt with a character that is normally a MS-DOS delimiter (blank space, semicolon, comma, etc.), precede the character with a null meta-string (a character that has no meaning to PROMPT, such as $A).

Meta-Strings

A *meta-string* is a group of characters transformed into another character or characters. To use certain characters (for example, the < or > I/O redirection symbols), you must enter the appropriate meta-string in order to place the desired character(s) in your *promptstring*. Otherwise,

MS-DOS immediately attempts to interpret the character.

All meta-strings begin with the dollar sign ($) and consist of two characters, including the $. The following list contains meta-string characters and their meanings:

Character	What It Produces
$	$, the dollar sign
_ (underscore)	New line, (moves to the first position of the next line)
b	l, the vertical *b*ar
d	The *d*ate, like the DATE command
e	The *e*scape character, CHR$(27)
g	>, the *g*reater-than character
h	The backspace character, CHR$(8), which erases the previous character
l	<, the *l*ess-than character
n	The curre*n*t disk drive
p	The current disk drive and *p*ath, including the current directory
q	=, the e*q*ual sign
t	The *t*ime, like the TIME command
v	The *v*ersion number of MS-DOS
Any other	Nothing or null; the character is ignored

Examples
1. **PROMPT**

    or

    PROMPT ng

PROMPT sets the MS-DOS system prompt to the normal prompt (A>). Here, the first example shows the default use of PROMPT. If you do not specify a *promptstring*, the standard system prompt is restored. In the second example the **$n** is the letter of the current disk drive, and the **$g** is the greater-than sign (>). The new prompt, if the current disk drive is A, becomes A + >, or A>.

2. **PROMPT The current drive is $n:**

This command sets the new system prompt to

```
The current drive is A:
```

3. **PROMPT $p**

PROMPT sets the system prompt to the current disk drive and the path to the current directory. If you are using the example disk in drive A and are in the SAMPLES directory, the system prompt in this command line displays

```
A:\MS-DOS\BASIC\SAMPLES
```

4. **PROMPT $A;$t;**

PROMPT sets the system prompt to the system time, such as

```
;12:04:12.46;
```

Note that a semicolon normally separates items on the MS-DOS command line. To make the first character of the system prompt a delimiter, a null meta-string must be used. Because $A does not have any special meaning for MS-DOS, the system ignores this meta-string and makes the semicolon the first character of the new prompt.

5. **PROMPT $$**

This sets the system prompt to imitate UNIX's Bourne shell prompt:

$

Notes

With hierarchical directories, displaying the current path on your disk drive is helpful. For that reason, many MS-DOS V3 users may want to set the system prompt to

PROMPT $p

This command displays the current disk drive and the current path as the prompt.

To cancel your new prompt and restore the old A> prompt, just reissue the PROMPT without a prompt-string.

═ **RECOVER** ═══════════════

(Recover files or disk directory)   *External*

Purpose

Recovers a file with bad sectors or a file from a disk with a damaged directory

Syntax

To recover a file, use:

*dc:pathc***RECOVER** *d:path\\filename.ext*

To recover a disk with a damaged directory, use:

   *dc:pathc*RECOVER d:

dc: is the name of the disk drive holding the command.

pathc is the path to the command.

d: is the name of the disk drive holding the damaged file or diskette.

path is the path to the directory holding the file to be recovered.

filename.ext is the file to be recovered. Wild cards are allowed, but only the first file that matches the wild-card file name is RECOVERed.

RENAME or REN

(Rename file)   *Internal*

Purpose

Changes the name of the disk file(s)

Syntax

RENAME *d:path*filename1.*ext1* filename2.*ext2*

or

REN *d:path*filename1.*ext1* filename2.*ext2*

d: is the name of the disk drive holding the file(s) to be renamed.

path is the path to the file(s) to be renamed.

filename1.*ext1* is the current name of the file. Wild cards are allowed.

filename2.*ext2* is the new name for the file. Wild cards are allowed.

REPLACE

(Replace/update files)   *External*

Purpose

Selectively replaces files with matching names from one disk to another. Selectively adds files from one disk to another.

Syntax

    *dc:pathc***REPLACE** *ds:paths***filenames.***exts*
     dd:pathd /A/P/R/S/W

dc: is the name of the disk drive holding the command.

pathc is the path to the command.

ds: is the name of the disk drive holding the replacement files.

paths is the path to the replacement files.

filenames.*exts* is the name of the replacement files. Wild cards are allowed.

dd: is the name of the disk drive holding the replacement files.

pathd is the path to the replacement files.

Terms

The file(s) that will be added to or that will replace another file(s) is the *source* represented by an *s* in the name (*ds:paths***filenames.***exts*).

The file(s) that will be replaced or the disk and directory that will have the file(s) added is the *destination*, represented by the letter *d* (*dd:pathd*). MS-DOS refers to this as the *target*.

Switches

/A *Add* files from sources that do not exist on the destination.

/P *Prompt* and ask whether the file should be replaced or added to the destination.

/R Replace *read-only* files also.

/S Replace files in the current directory and allow *subdirectories* beneath this directory.

/W *Wait* for the source diskette to be inserted.

RESTORE

(Restore backed up files)   *External*

Purpose

Restores one or more backup files from a diskette or hard disk onto another diskette or hard disk. This command complements the BACKUP command.

Syntax

RESTORE d1: *d2:path\filename.ext* /S /P /M /N /B:date /A:date /L:time /E:time

d1: is the name of the disk drive holding the backup file(s).

d2: is the disk drive to receive the restored file(s).

path is the path name of the path to the directory to receive the restored file(s).

filename.ext is the name of the file you want to restore.

Wild cards are allowed.

Switches

/S   Restores files in the directory specified and all other *subdirectories* below it. This switch is identical to BACKUP's /S switch.

/P   *Prompts* and asks whether a file should be restored if it is marked as read-only or has been changed since the last backup.

/N   Restores all files that *no longer* exist on the destination. This switch is like the /M switch, but /N processes only the files deleted from the destination since the backup set was made. This switch is new in MS-DOS V3.3.

/M   Restores all files *modified* or deleted since the backup set was made. This switch is like the /N switch because /M processes files that no longer exist on the destination, but /M also restores files that have been modified since the last backup. This switch is new in MS-DOS V3.3.

/A:date   Restores all files created or modified on or *after* the *date*. The format of *date* is the same as the /B switch. This switch is new in MS-DOS V3.3.

/B:date   Restores all files created or modified on or *before* the *date*. This switch is new in MS-DOS V3.3.

/L:time   Restores all files modified at or *later* than the specified *time*. The form of time is *hh:mm:ss*, where *hh* is the hour; *mm*, the minutes; and *ss*, the seconds. This switch is new in MS-DOS V3.3.

E/:time Restores all files modified at or *earlier* than the specified *time*. This switch is new in MS-DOS V3.3.

RMDIR or RD

(Remove directory)   *Internal*

Purpose

Removes a subdirectory

Syntax

RMDIR *d:*path

or

RD *d:*path

d: is the name of the drive holding the subdirectory.

path is the name of the path to the subdirectory. The last path name is the subdirectory you want to delete.

SELECT

(Select country configuration)   *External*

Syntax

*dc:pathc*SELECT *ds: dd:pathd* countrycode keycode

dc: is the name of the disk drive holding the command.

pathc is the path to the command.

ds: is the name of the disk drive holding the MS-DOS files— the *source* disk drive (A: or B:).

dd: is the name of the disk drive to be formatted and that will receive the appropriate MS-DOS files—the destination disk drive.

pathd is the path to the subdirectory that will receive the appropriate MS-DOS files—the *destination* directory.

countrycode is the country code.

keycode is the keyboard code.

SET

(Set/show environment)   *Internal*

Purpose

Sets or shows the system environment

Syntax

To display the environment, use:

    SET

To add to or alter the environment, use:

    SET name=*string*

name is the name of the string you want to add to the environment.

string is the information you want to store in the environment.

Terms

The *environment* is an area in RAM memory reserved for alphanumeric information that may be examined and used by MS-DOS commands or user programs. For example, the environment usually contains COMSPEC, the location of COMMAND.COM; PATH, the additional paths for finding programs and batch files; and PROMPT, the string defining the MS-DOS system prompt.

SETUP

(Set computer parameters)   *External*

Purpose

Allows you to set or change specific computer system parameters

Syntax

SETUP

Notes

SETUP is an MS-DOS program that most users will use only once while they have their computers.

Generally, SETUP allows you to specify system constraints for your computer. Some parameters that SETUP usually controls include the number and type of disk drives attached to your computer, the type and number of video monitors, and the amount of RAM (and how the RAM is used).

Since the specifics of what SETUP allows you to do will differ from computer to computer, consult your computer operator's manual for more specific information.

SHARE

(Check shared files)   *External*

Purpose

Enables MS-DOS support for file and record locking

Syntax

*dc:pathc***SHARE** */F:name_space /L:numlocks*

dc: is the name of the disk drive holding the command.

pathc is the path to the command.

Switches

/F :name_space   Sets the amount of memory space
(name_space bytes large) used for file
sharing

/L:numlocks   Sets the maximum number (numlocks)
of file/record locks to use.

Rules

1. If you do not give the /F switch, *name_space* is set
    to 2,048 bytes. Each open file uses 11 bytes plus its
    full file specification (disk drive name, path name,
    and file name). The 2,048 bytes can contain 27 files
    that use all 63 characters available for the full file
    name.

2. If you do not give the /L switch, a default of 20
    simultaneous file locks is allowed.

3. When SHARE is loaded, MS-DOS checks each file
    for file and record locks during the opening,
    reading, and writing of the file.

4. SHARE should be loaded only once after MS-DOS
    has started. If you attempt to load SHARE again,
    MS-DOS displays an error message.

5. SHARE normally increases the size of MS-DOS by
    approximately 4,900 bytes. If the number of locks
    (/L switch) or memory space (/F switch) is
    increased or decreased, the size of MS-DOS also
    increases or decreases proportionately.

6. The only way to remove SHARE is to restart
    MS-DOS.

7. If you have not given the FCBS command in your
    CONFIG.SYS file, SHARE adjusts the file control
    block (FCB) table as if the command FCBS = 16,8
    were given.

Notes

SHARE is the MS-DOS V3 program for file and record locking.

You use SHARE when two or more programs or processes share the files of a single computer. After SHARE is loaded, MS-DOS checks each file for locks whenever it is opened, read, or written. If a file has been opened for exclusive use, a second attempt to open the file produces an error. If one program locks a portion of a file, another program attempting to read, write, or read and write the locked portion creates an error.

SHARE affects two or more programs running on the same computer, not two or more computers using the same file (networked computers). File and record locking for two or more computers using the same file is made possible by software provided with the network.

SORT

(Sort string filter)   *External*

Purpose

Reads lines from the standard input device, performs an ASCII sort of the lines, and then writes the lines to the standard output device. The sorting may be in ascending or descending order and may start at any column in the line.

Syntax

   *dc:pathc***SORT** */R /+c*

   dc: is the name of the disk drive holding the command.

   pathc is the path to the command.

Switches

   /R   Sorts in reverse order. Thus, the letter Z comes first, and the letter A comes last.

/+c   Starts sorting with column number c.

Examples

   1.   **SORT <WORDS.TXT**

   SORT sorts the lines in the file WORDS.TXT and
   displays the sorted lines on the video screen.

   2.   **SORT <WORDS.TXT /R**

   SORT sorts in reverse order the lines in the file
   WORDS.TXT and displays the lines on the video
   screen.

   3.   **SORT /+8 <WORDS.TXT**

   SORT starts sorting at the eighth character in each line
   of WORDS.TXT and displays the output on the video
   display.

   4.   **DIR | SORT /+14**

   SORT displays the directory information sorted by file
   size. (The file size starts in the 14th column.) Unfortunately, other lines, such as the volume label, are also
   sorted starting at the 14th column.

SUBST

(Substitute path name)   *External*

Purpose

   Creates an alias disk drive name for a subdirectory; used
   principally with programs that do not use path names.

Syntax

   To establish an alias, use:

   dc:pathc**SUBST d1: d2:pathname**

To delete an alias, use:

   dc:pathc**SUBST d1: /D**

To see the current aliases, use:

   dc:pathc**SUBST**

dc: is the name of the disk drive holding the command.

pathc\\ is the path to the command.

d1: is a valid disk drive name that becomes the alias (or nickname). **d1:** may be a nonexistent disk drive.

d2:pathname is the valid disk drive name and directory path that will be nicknamed **d1:**.

___
Switch
   /D Deletes the alias

___
Examples
   a.   **SUBST E: C:\BIN**

When you use disk drive name E, the directory C:\BIN is actually used.

   b.   **SUBST F: C:LETTERS**

Drive F is substituted for the directory C:\WORDS \LETTERS. Because the current directory of drive C was \WORDS, MS-DOS found LETTERS as the subdirectory of WORDS. MS-DOS adds \WORDS\ to the alias.

   c.   **SUBST**

Shows the current aliases. SUBST displays

```
E: => C:\BIN
F: => C:\WORDS\LETTERS
```

d.   **SUBST F: /D**

The alias **F:** is deleted. Afterward, the use of **F:**
produces an error message from MS-DOS.

SYS

(Place the operating system on the disk)

External

Purpose

Places a copy of MS-DOS on the specified diskette or
hard disk

Syntax

dc:pathc\ **SYS d:**

dc: is the name of the disk drive holding the command.

pathc is the path to the command.

d: is the disk drive to receive the copy of MS-DOS.

Rules

1. You must specify the name of the disk drive to
    receive a copy of MS-DOS.

2. The disk to receive the copy of MS-DOS must
    conform to one of the following conditions:

    a. Be formatted with the */S* option (MS-DOS V1,
        V2, or V3)

    b. Be formatted with the */B* option (MS-DOS V2 or
        V3)

    c. Be completely empty

    d. Be formatted with a special program that
        reserves the proper disk space for the operating
        system

If you attempt to put the system on a disk that does not meet one of these conditions, a No room for system on destination disk message appears, and MS-DOS does not perform the operation.

3. A copy of MS-DOS (the IO.SYS and MSDOS.SYS files) should reside on the current disk. Otherwise, you will be asked to insert in the floppy disk drive a diskette containing these files.

4. You cannot use SYS on a networked disk drive.

Notes

The SYS command places a copy of IO.SYS and MSDOS.SYS on the targeted disk. To make the disk bootable (able to load and execute the disk operating system), you must also copy COMMAND.COM.

The SYS command puts MS-DOS on applications program diskettes sold without MS-DOS. With these diskettes, you can boot the computer system by using the applications software. A diskette provided by the program publisher must be specially formatted, however, or SYS will not work. You should check the instructions that come with the application program to see whether you can put the system on the diskette.

TIME

(Set/show the time)   *Internal*

Purpose

Sets and shows the system time

Syntax

TIME *hh:mm:ss.xx*

hh is the one- or two-digit number for hours (0 to 23).

mm is the one- or two-digit number for minutes (0 to 60).

ss is the one- or two-digit number for seconds (0 to 60).

xx is the one- or two-digit number for hundredths of a second (0 to 99).

Note: Depending on the setting of the country code in your CONFIG.SYS file, a comma may be the separator between seconds and hundredths of seconds.

TREE

(Display all directories)   *External*

Purpose

Displays all the subdirectories on a disk and optionally displays all the files in each directory

Syntax

*dc:pathc***TREE** *d:* /F

dc: is the name of the disk drive holding the command.

pathc is the path to the command.

d: is the name of the disk drive holding the disk you want to examine.

Switch

/F Displays all files in the directories

TYPE

(Type file on screen)   *Internal*

Purpose

Displays the contents of the file on the screen

d: is the name of the disk drive holding the file to TYPE.

path is the MS-DOS path to the file.

filename.*ext* is the name of the file to TYPE. Wild cards are not permitted.

═ VER

(Display version number)   Internal

Purpose

Shows the MS-DOS version number on the video display

Syntax

VER

Notes

The VER command shows the one-digit version number, followed by a two-digit revision number. You can determine which MS-DOS version (V2.0 through V3.31 or later) the computer is using. If you type the line

VER

you will see a message similar to this:

```
COMPAQ Personal Computer
 DOS Version 3.31
```

If you see a Bad command or file name message, you are working with MS-DOS V1.

VERIFY

(Set/show disk verification)   *Internal*

Purpose

Sets the computer to check the accuracy of data written
to the disk(s) to ensure that information is properly
recorded, and shows whether the data has been checked

Syntax

To show the verify status, use:

    VERIFY

To set the verify status, use:

    VERIFY ON

    or

    VERIFY OFF

Rules

1. VERIFY accepts only one of two parameters: ON
   or OFF.

2. Once VERIFY is ON, it remains on until one of the
   following occurs:

   a. A VERIFY OFF is issued.

   b. A SET VERIFY system call turns off the
      command.

   c. MS-DOS is restarted.

Notes

VERIFY controls new data checking on the disk to
ensure that the data has been correctly recorded. If
VERIFY is off, MS-DOS does not check the data. If

VERIFY is on, MS-DOS checks the data. VERIFY does not affect any other MS-DOS operation.

Two factors affect the tradeoff between VERIFY ON and VERIFY OFF. If VERIFY is on, data integrity is assured. If VERIFY is off, you can write to the disk faster. You are usually safe to leave VERIFY off if you are not working with critical information (such as a company's accounting figures). You are wise to turn VERIFY on when you are backing up your hard disk or making important copies on the diskettes.

The degree of performance lost in verifying is different for the hard disk and for diskettes. On the average, MS-DOS takes 68 percent more time to verify information written on the hard disk. This percentage is radically different for MS-DOS V2, which takes only 8 to 9 percent more time. On the average, MS-DOS V3 takes 100 percent more time when verifying information written to the diskette. MS-DOS V2 takes about 90 percent.

VOL

(Display volume label)   *Internal*

Purpose

Displays the volume label of the disk, if the label exists

Syntax

VOL *d:*

d: is the name of the disk drive whose label you want to display.

Rules

If you do not give a disk drive name, the current disk drive is used.

XCOPY

(Extended COPY)   *External*

Purpose

Selectively copies files from one or more subdirectories

Syntax

*dc:pathc***XCOPY** *ds:paths\\filenames.exts dd:pathd*
filenamed.extd /A /D /E /M /P /S /V /W

dc: is the name of the disk drive holding the command.

pathc is the path to the command.

ds: is the name of the disk drive holding the files to be
copied.

paths is the path to the files to be copied.

filenames.exts is the name of the file(s) to be copied.
Wild cards are allowed.

dd: is the name of the disk drive that will receive the
copied files—this is the destination (MS-DOS refers to
it as the target).

pathd is the path that will receive the copied files.

filenamed.extd is the name to be given to the copied
files. Wild cards are allowed.

Switches

/V	*Verifies* that the files have been copied correctly (identical to COPY's /V switch).
/W	*Waits* until the disk has been changed. XCOPY prompts you to change diskettes before it searches for the files to copy.

/P   *Pauses* and asks for confirmation before
            copying each file.

/S   Copies the files in the source directory
            and all files in subsequent *subdirectories*.
            This option is identical to BACKUP's
            and RESTORE's /S switch.

/E   When given with the /S switch, causes
            XCOPY to create *empty* subdirectories on
            the destination if the subdirectory on the
            source is empty. If you do not give the /E
            switch, /S ignores empty directories.

/A   Copies files with *archive* flags set to on
            (the file has been created or modified
            since the last running of BACKUP or
            XCOPY). /A does not reset the file's
            archive flag.

/M   Copies files with archive flags set to on
            (the file has been created or *modified*
            since the last running of BACKUP or
            XCOPY). /M resets the file's archive
            flag.

/D:*date*   Copies files created or modified since
            date. This option is identical to
            BACKUP's /D switch.

Batch Files

A batch file provides a shortcut for executing one or many MS-DOS commands. When you type just the name of a batch file, the file executes each line as if you had entered the line from the keyboard.

Batch files can automate long or repetitive instructions. The chance of mistyping a command is reduced, and long tasks can be started and left to run unattended.

Writing batch files can be viewed as a way of programming in MS-DOS. This section indicates the procedure for creating batch files, explains the batch subcommands, and gives examples of batch files you can use.

Creating Batch Files

You can create batch files by using COPY CON, any word processor capable of creating text files (most can), or a text editor (including the MS-DOS EDLIN editor). COPY CON is not recommended for the longer examples because of the inconvenience in correcting typing errors.

If you use a word processor, use the programmer, ASCII key or nondocument, mode. The normal mode of many word processors stores the characters you type in a code that MS-DOS may not understand. If your word-processing program doesn't distinguish between documents and nondocuments, use the following method to create a test batch file.

1. Type a simple batch file like those explained in this section. Each line of the file must be a single executable MS-DOS command. Avoid underlining, bold, and other special formatting. Be sure that no hard return or other symbols appear on-screen.

2. Save the batch file with a file extension of BAT; then try to run it at the MS-DOS prompt.

3. If a `Bad Command or File Name` message appears, check the index of your word processor's manual to look up ASCII files to see how the program stores files in ASCII or non-document mode. If no information is available, call the software publisher to ask how to write batch files with the program.

The batch files given in this section are typed in all capital letters. MS-DOS accepts lowercase letters except in special cases that are pointed out in the text.

Rules for Creating Batch Files

1. A batch file contains ASCII text. You may create a batch file by using the MS-DOS command COPY, EDLIN (a line editor), or another text editor. If you use a word-processing program, make sure that it is in programming, or nondocument, mode when you create the batch file.

2. The batch file's root name can be from one to eight characters long and must conform to the rules for creating file names.

3. The file name extension must be .BAT.

4. A batch file should not have the same root name as that of a program file (a file ending with .COM and .EXE) in the current directory. Nor should you use an internal MS-DOS command, such as COPY or DATE, as a root name. If you use one of these root names to name a batch file, and then try to run the batch file, MS-DOS will execute the program or the command instead.

5. You may enter any valid MS-DOS system-level commands. You also may use the parameter

markers (%0-%9), environmental variables by enclosing the variable name in percent signs (such as **%COMSPEC%**), and the batch subcommands.

6. You may enter any valid batch subcommand.

7. To use the percent sign (%) for a file name in a command, enter the percent symbol twice. For example, to use a file called A100%.TXT, you enter **A100%%.TXT**. This rule does not apply to the parameter markers (0%-9%) or environmental variables.

8. You may suppress the display of any line from the batch file if an @ is the first nonspace character on the line.

Executing Batch Files

You execute a batch file by entering the batch-file name at the MS-DOS prompt, using the following syntax:

   *dc:pathc***filename** *parameters*

dc: is the name of the disk drive that holds the batch file.

pathc is the path to the batch file.

filename is the batch file's root name.

parameters are the parameters to be used by the batch file.

Rules for Executing Batch Files

1. A batch file must have the extension .BAT.

2. If you do not give a disk drive name, the current disk drive is used.

3. If you do not give a path name, the current directory is used.

4. To invoke a batch file, simply type its root name. For example, to invoke the batch file OFTEN.BAT, type **OFTEN**, and then press Enter.

5. MS-DOS executes each command one line at a time. The specified parameters are substituted for the markers when the command is used.

6. MS-DOS recognizes a maximum of ten parameters. You may use the SHIFT subcommand to get around this limitation.

7. If MS-DOS encounters an incorrectly phrased batch subcommand when you run a batch file, it displays a Syntax error message, and then continues with the remaining commands in the batch file.

8. You can stop a running batch file by pressing Ctrl-Break. MS-DOS will display this message:

```
Terminate batch job (Y/N)?_
```

If you answer **Y** for yes, the rest of the commands are ignored, and the system prompt appears. If you answer **N** for no, MS-DOS skips the current command but continues to process the other commands in the file.

9. MS-DOS remembers which directory holds the batch file. Your batch file may cause the current directory to change at any time.

10. MS-DOS remembers which diskette holds the batch file, and you may change diskettes at any time. MS-DOS will prompt you to insert the diskette that holds the batch file, if necessary. However, for V3.0, if the batch file is on a diskette, you may not remove the diskette. If you remove it, MS-DOS

displays an error message and stops processing the batch file.

11. You can make MS-DOS execute a second batch file immediately after the first one is finished. Simply enter the name of the second batch file as the last command in the first batch file. You can also execute a second batch file within the first batch file and return to the first batch file by using the CALL subcommand.

12. Batch subcommands are valid only for batch files. You cannot execute batch-file subcommands as normal MS-DOS commands.

13. You may not redirect the input or output of a batch file. However, you can use redirection in the lines within a batch file.

Rules for AUTOEXEC.BAT

1. The file must be called AUTOEXEC.BAT and reside in the boot disk's root directory.

2. The AUTOEXEC.BAT file's contents must conform to the rules for creating batch files.

3. When you boot MS-DOS, MS-DOS automatically executes the AUTOEXEC.BAT file.

4. When MS-DOS executes the AUTOEXEC.BAT file after the computer boots, the system doesn't automatically request the date and time. To get the current date and time, you must put the DATE and TIME commands in the AUTOEXEC.BAT file.

Starting a Program with a Batch File

The sequence of directory commands leading up to the running of a particular program can be automated by placing them in a batch file. As a simple example, suppose that you regularly start a program called APPLIQUE from a particular directory. You call up the program, copy some files after you exit from the program, and then jump back to the root directory. You can set up a batch file that contains the following lines (assume that the hard disk is drive C):

```
C:
CD \APPDATA
APPLIQUE
COPY *.DAT B:
CD \
```

If you named the batch file A.BAT, type an a and press Enter when you want MS-DOS to execute the series of commands in the file.

You do not need to type an extension.

When you type a and press Enter, MS-DOS looks in the current directory for a file named A.COM, A.EXE, or A.BAT, in that order. Provided that you do not have A.COM or A.EXE in your directory, MS-DOS runs the batch file A.BAT. As the batch file runs, you can see the commands appear on-screen and then execute one-by-one.

Remember that MS-DOS executes only files with extensions of COM, EXE, and BAT. If you try to execute a command using any extension but these three, MS-DOS cannot find a file the program can execute, and therefore displays the error message:

```
Bad command or file name
```

Using CLS to Clear the Screen

One goal of batch-file creators is to keep a screen clean. Some people prefer not to see even the first ECHO OFF when a batch file starts. Unfortunately, because batch

files start with an implicit ECHO ON command, you
cannot stop the first ECHO OFF statement from being
displayed. However, you can use a trick that almost
eliminates the display. With V3.2 or lower, you can start
the batch file with the following command:

```
ECHO OFF
CLS
```

CLS is the MS-DOS clear-screen command built into
COMMAND.COM. Although not a batch subcommand,
CLS has an excellent use in batch files. When CLS
immediately follows ECHO OFF, the screen clears so
quickly that you see the ECHO OFF only if you look for
it. If you are using MS-DOS V3.3, @CLS should appear
first, followed by @ECHO OFF. This refreshes the
screen more quickly. If you want only to turn off ECHO
without first clearing the screen, you can use just the
second statement.

Defining Parameters

The information you type after the command is called a
parameter. Within a batch file, you can define up to 10
parameters. You define a parameter within the batch file
by using a *variable marker*; a variable is the percent sign
(%) followed by a number from 0 to 9. Variables are
called markers, replaceable parameters, or arguments.

Examples

Example 1. Consider the file MOVE.BAT. This batch
file copies a file to a designated subdirectory and then
erases the original file:

```
COPY C:\%1 C:\SUBDIR1 /V
ERASE C:\%1
```

Suppose that you type the following command line:

```
MOVE FORMAT.COM
```

The batch file MOVE.BAT begins executing and
substitutes the first parameter (FORMAT.COM) for the
variable %1. After the substitution, the lines in the batch
file change to the following:

```
COPY C:\FORMAT.COM C:\SUBDIR1 /V
ERASE C:\FORMAT.COM
```

MS-DOS changes each %1 to the first parameter from
the command line.

If FORMAT.COM is located in the C drive root
directory, the MOVE batch file copies FORMAT.COM
(with verification) to the subdirectory called SUBDIR1
and then erases FORMAT.COM from the root. This
batch file saves you the extra step of erasing the original
file after it has been copied.

Example 2. You can make the MOVE batch file more
general by setting up two parameters: one for the file
name and the second for the disk or directory to which
the file will move. By using the second parameter, you
can direct MS-DOS to copy the file to any subdirectory
on drive C. This new batch file is simple:

```
COPY C:\%1 C:\%2 /V
ERASE C:\%1
```

Then, to move the file FORMAT.COM to the directory
C:\DOS31, type the following:

```
MOVE FORMAT.COM DOS31
```

This batch file contains a major flaw. What if you
mistype or omit the directory name, the second
parameter? At the COPY command, MS-DOS issues an
Invalid directory message and does not copy the file.
The danger is that MS-DOS proceeds to the next step of
erasing the file. The original file has not been copied but
is erased!

In the same way, if you forget to type any second parameter, MS-DOS issues the error message `File cannot be copied onto itself` and does not copy the file. Even so, the second line causes MS-DOS to erase the file. The earlier MOVE.BAT file did not encounter this problem because a valid subdirectory name for the destination (SUBDIR1) was embedded in the batch file.

Counting Parameters

A batch file has 10 possible parameters: %0 through %9. The first parameter is parameter number 0 and is designated as %0 in batch files. The parameter %0 signifies the name of the batch file you typed at the MS-DOS prompt.

The remaining items on the line are parameters 1 through 9. The first word after the batch-file name is parameter number 1, %1 in the file. The second word is %2, and the ninth item on the line is %9. Each word on the line is separated from the next by a space, comma, colon, semicolon, single quotation mark, or equal sign.

When you use replaceable parameters, remember you should start with %1, not with %0.

Although MS-DOS restricts you to parameters 0 to 9 within a batch file, a command line can have many parameters within the command line's 127-character limit. See the explanation of the SHIFT subcommand to learn how to trick MS-DOS into using the other arguments.

Using Batch File Commands

You can use any valid MS-DOS command in a batch file. MS-DOS also has a set of commands specifically for use in batch files: the batch subcommands. The batch subcommands for V3 are listed on the following page.

Command	Operation
@	Suppresses the display of a line on-screen (MS-DOS V3.3 and later)
CALL	Runs another batch file and then returns to the original batch file (MS-DOS V3.3 and later)
ECHO	Turns on or off the display of batch commands and displays a message on the screen
FOR..IN..DO	Allows the use of the same batch command for several files
GOTO	Jumps to the line after a label in the batch file
IF	Allows conditional execution of a command
PAUSE	Halts processing until a key is pressed and optionally displays a message
REM	Displays a message on the screen
SHIFT	Shifts the command line parameters one parameter to the left

CALL

Batch Subcommand

Purpose

Runs a second batch file, and then returns control to the first batch file

Syntax

CALL *dc:pathc*filename *parameters*

dc: is the name of the disk drive that holds the called batch file.

pathc is the path to the called batch file.

filename is the root name of the called batch file.

parameters are the parameters to be used by the batch file.

Rules

1. If you do not give a disk drive name, the current disk drive is used.

2. If you do not give a path name, the current directory is used.

3. The named batch file is run as if invoked from the keyboard. Parameters are passed to the called batch file as if the file were invoked from the keyboard.

4. You may not redirect the input or output of the batch file that you have called using CALL. However, you can use redirection on the lines within the batch file which you have called.

5. When the second batch file finishes, MS-DOS executes the next line of the first batch file.

Notes

Use the CALL command to run a second batch file from another batch file. When the second batch file is finished, MS-DOS continues processing the remaining commands in the first batch file.

If CALL is not used to run the second batch file, MS-DOS concludes batch-file processing when the second file finishes. MS-DOS does not normally return to the first batch file.

You can duplicate the same procedure in versions of MS-DOS prior to V3.3 by using COMMAND in the form

COMMAND /C *dc:pathc*\filename *parameters*

where filename is the root name of the second batch file.

ECHO

Batch Subcommand

Purpose

Displays a message and allows or inhibits the display of batch commands and messages by other batch subcommands as MS-DOS executes these subcommands

Syntax

To display a message, use

ECHO *message*

To turn off the display of commands and messages by other batch commands, use

ECHO OFF

To turn on the display of commands and messages, use

ECHO ON

To see the status of ECHO, use

ECHO

message is the text of the message to be displayed on the video screen.

Rules

1. For unconditional display of a message on the video screen, use **ECHO** *message*.

2. When ECHO is on, the batch file displays each command as MS-DOS executes each line. The batch file also displays any messages from the batch subcommands.

3. When ECHO is off, the batch file does not display its commands as MS-DOS executes them. The batch file also does not display messages produced by other batch subcommands. The exceptions to this rule are the `Strike a key when ready` message generated by the PAUSE subcommand and any **ECHO** *message* command.

4. MS-DOS starts the system with ECHO on.

5. An ECHO OFF command is active until batch processing is finished or an ECHO ON command is encountered. If one batch file invokes another, ECHO is not turned back on by MS-DOS when the second batch file is invoked. ECHO is turned on after the final batch file is processed.

6. ECHO affects messages produced only by batch subcommands. The command does not affect messages from other MS-DOS commands or programs.

Example

This example uses the ECHO command to display messages:

```
ECHO OFF
ECHO To run this program, make sure
ECHO the disk containing BASICA is
```

ECHO in drive A and the disk labeled
ECHO CONTRACTS is in drive B.
ECHO _____
ECHO (If you need to exit at this time,
ECHO hold down the Ctrl key and press
ECHO the Break key. When the system
ECHO asks you whether you want to
ECHO "Terminate batch job (Y/N)?"
ECHO press Y. The batch file will stop.)

The first command, ECHO OFF, is the "noise
suppressor." ECHO OFF suppresses the *echoing*
(displaying) of any batch commands on-screen as that
command is executed. However, ECHO OFF does not
turn off messages displayed by another ECHO
command. ECHO OFF turns off REM statements but
not other ECHO statements. Running the preceding
chunk of a batch file produces the following display:

```
C>ECHO OFF
To run this program, make sure
the disk containing BASICA is
in drive A and the disk labeled
CONTRACTS is in drive B.
_____
(If you need to exit at this time,
hold down the Ctrl key and press
the Break key. When the system
asks you whether you want to
"Terminate batch job (Y/N)?"
press Y. The batch file will stop.)
```

To see the differences between the ECHO and REM,
create the batch file using REM and execute the file.
Then create the version using ECHO (or edit the old
batch file) and execute this file. Using ECHO OFF and
an ECHO message gives neat and informative messages;
using REM with ECHO ON gives operational clutter
that can confuse novice users or distract frequent users.

Both ECHO and REM statements are useful in a batch file. With ECHO OFF, REM protects comments that you want to remain in the batch file but do not want to appear on-screen and ECHO displays messages on-screen. REM comments can serve as documentation when you or others want to change the file later, and ECHO messages can provide on-screen guidance.

With ECHO ON, ECHO statements appear twice and REM statements appear once.

Notes

The ECHO message is not the same as the REM message. REM is affected by an ECHO OFF command. The message on the line with the REM subcommand is not displayed if ECHO is off. The message on the line with ECHO is always displayed.

You can suppress the display of a single batch-file line by using the @ as the first character in a line. By using the line

@ECHO OFF

the command ECHO OFF is not displayed on the screen.

The implicit ECHO ON of batch files differs between MS-DOS V2 and later versions. With MS-DOS V2, when the first batch file runs another batch file, ECHO is automatically turned back on, regardless of whether ECHO was turned off by the preceding batch file. MS-DOS V2 batch files must have an ECHO OFF statement in every batch file to keep ECHO turned off.

With MS-DOS V3, once ECHO is turned off, it stays off until the batch files are finished or an ECHO ON command is given. All subsequent batch files are silent. This property of ECHO is important when batch files run each other. This aspect, however, does not apply when you manually run more than one batch file. Once any batch file returns to MS-DOS, ECHO is reset.

Finally, be sure to use ECHO OFF only within batch files. If you type ECHO OFF at the prompt, the prompt itself becomes invisible, cursor and all.

To suppress the output of a command, use I/O redirection to the null device (NUL). For example, to suppress the file(s) copied message when you are using COPY, use the form:

COPY file1.ext file2.ext >NUL

The command's output is sent to the null device and is not displayed on the screen.

FOR..IN..DO

Batch Subcommand

Purpose

Allows iterative (repeated) processing of an MS-DOS command

Syntax

FOR %%variable IN (set) DO command

variable is a single letter.

set is one or more words or file specifications. The file specification is in the form *d:path***filename**.*ext*. Wildcards are allowed.

command is the MS-DOS command to be performed for each word or file in the set.

Rules

1. You may use more than one word or a full file specification in the **set**. Separate words or file specifications by spaces or by commas.

2. %%variable becomes each literal word or full file specification in the set. If you use wildcard characters, FOR..IN..DO executes once for each file that matches the wildcard file specification.

3. You may use path names.

4. You cannot nest FOR..IN..DO subcommands (put two of these subcommands on the same line). You may use other batch subcommands with FOR..IN..DO.

5. Wildcards (* or ?) in file names are valid in this command.

Examples

Example 1. The following batch file shows a simple example of FOR..IN..DO that gets a directory listing for each file in the directory:

FOR %%a IN (*.*) DO DIR %%a

For every file that matches the name *.* (all files), MS-DOS does a DIR command (directory list) using the names of the matching files. If the directory holds COMMAND .COM, AUTOEXEC.BAT, and CONFIG .SYS, MS-DOS expands the batch-file line in the following manner:

FOR %%a IN (COMMAND.COM
AUTOEXEC.BAT CONFIG.SYS) DO DIR %%a
DIR COMMAND.COM
DIR AUTOEXEC.BAT
DIR CONFIG.SYS

MS-DOS executes the DIR command once for each file in the set. Each time the command is executed, MS-DOS substitutes for the %%a an item from the set. In this case, the DIR command is executed three times sequentially using the names in the set. In sequence,

%%a is replaced by COMMAND.COM, AUTOEXEC
.BAT, and CONFIG.SYS.

This batch file is simplistic and impractical because a
single DIR command shows a listing for all files in the
directory. However, the file is an example of how
FOR..IN..DO works.

Example 2. This example uses FOR..IN..DO in a batch
file called FORMAT.BAT that allows you to format
only drive A: or drive B:.

```
ECHO OFF
IF %1. == . GOTO NONE
FOR %%a IN (a:, A:, b:, B:) DO IF %1 ==
   %%a GOTO FORMAT
ECHO You don't really mean to format %1,
   do you?
GOTO END
:NONE
ECHO You did not specify the drive (B), e.g.
FORMAT B:
ECHO Please try the command again.
GOTO END
:FORMAT
XFORMAT   %1
:END
```

This batch file first tests for an empty parameter %1
because MS-DOS gives errors when testing anything
against an empty string. The next command tests
whether the designated disk drive is A or B, in both
upper- and lowercase versions. If the letters match,
processing jumps to where the file invokes the
FORMAT command. If no match is found, processing
drops to an error message and then jumps to END.

Notes

For the FOR..IN..DO subcommand, MS-DOS V2 does
not allow path names, but MS-DOS V3 does.

set can also contain literal words, separated by spaces.
set replaces % %variable when the command executes.

GOTO

Batch Subcommand

Purpose

Jumps (transfers control) to the line following the label
in the batch file and continues batch-file execution from
that line

Syntax

GOTO label

label is the name used for one or more characters,
preceded by a colon. Only the first eight characters of
the label name are significant.

Rules

1. The label must be the first item on a line in a batch
   file and must start with a colon (:).

2. When **GOTO label** is executed, MS-DOS jumps to
   the line following the label and continues execution
   of the batch file.

3. A **label** is never executed. MS-DOS uses the label
   only as the jump-to marker for the GOTO
   subcommand.

4. If you issue a GOTO command with a nonexistent
   label, MS-DOS issues an error message and stops
   processing the batch file.

Example

This sample batch file uses GOTO and a label:

```
:START
DIR B:
```

        PAUSE
        GOTO START

As the first character in the line, the colon designates
that the name START is a label. When this batch file is
run, MS-DOS displays a list of the files on drive B and
pauses. The final line directs MS-DOS to go to the
:START line and execute the batch file again.

This perpetual batch file continues until you stop the
action by pressing the Ctrl-Break or Ctrl-C key
combination. (It isn't elegant to stop a batch-file
execution by using Ctrl-Break unless absolutely
necessary.)

IF

Batch Subcommand

Purpose

Allows conditional execution of an MS-DOS command

Syntax

        IF *NOT* condition command

NOT tests for the opposite of the condition (executes the
command if the condition is false).

condition is what is being tested. It may be one of the
following:

        ERRORLEVEL number—MS-DOS tests the exit
        code (0 to 255) of the program. If the exit code is
        greater than or equal to the number, the condition is
        true.

        string1 == string2—MS-DOS tests whether these
        two alphanumeric strings are identical.

        EXIST *d:path*\filename.*ext*—MS-DOS tests
        whether the file *d:path*\filename.*ext* is in the

specified drive or path (if you give a drive name or path name), or is on the current disk drive and directory.

command is any valid MS-DOS command or batch subcommand except another IF statement. You cannot put two or more IF subcommands on the same line.

Rules

1. For the IF subcommand, if the condition is true, the command is executed. If the condition is false, the command is skipped, and the next line of the batch file is immediately executed.

2. For the IF NOT subcommand, if the condition is false, the command is executed. If the condition is true, the command is skipped, and the next line of the batch file is immediately executed.

3. The only MS-DOS programs that leave exit codes are BACKUP, FORMAT, GRAFTABL, KEYB, REPLACE, and RESTORE. Using an ERROR-LEVEL condition with a program that does not leave an exit code is meaningless.

4. For string1 == string2, MS-DOS makes a literal, character-by-character comparison of the two strings. The comparison is based on the ASCII character set, and upper- and lowercase letters are distinguished.

5. When you are using string1 == string2 with the parameter markers (%0;nd%9), neither string may be null . If either string is null, MS-DOS displays a Syntax error message and aborts the batch file.

Examples

Example 1. Checking existence.

This example uses IF in a batch file (MOVE.BAT) that copies a file from the root directory to a subdirectory

and then erases the file from the root directory. The IF
command first checks to see if the file you want to move
exists in the root directory:

```
IF NOT EXIST C:\%1 GOTO EXIT
COPY C:\%1 C:\SUBDIR1 /V
ERASE C:\%1
:EXIT
```

If the specified file (%1) does not exist in the root
directory, the batch file jumps (the GOTO command) to
the EXIT label and ends. If the file does exist, the file
executes the COPY and MOVE commands.

It might seem easier to test for a true condition (the
existence of a file) and then copy and erase the file, but
MS-DOS cannot control two or more commands with
IF. The alternative is to test for the opposite: "Does the
file not exist?" If the answer is true, the file skips the
COPY and ERASE commands. If the answer is false
(the file exists), execution drops through the IF
statement to the following lines and executes the COPY
and MOVE commands.

Note that execution always reaches the :EXIT label
regardless of the IF test. When a label is the next line to
execute, MS-DOS ignores the line and moves to the
following line. Labels have meaning only as targets of
GOTO statements; otherwise, MS-DOS treats labels as
harmless "noise."

If you want to get fancier, you can extend MOVE.BAT
again by having the batch file display a "file does not
exist" message, as in the following command:

```
ECHO OFF
CLS
IF NOT EXIST C:\%1 GOTO ERROR1
COPY C:\%1 C:\SUBDIR1 /V
ERASE C:\%1
GOTO EXIT :ERROR1
```

ECHO The file (%1) does not exist...
:EXIT

The third line performs the test for a file's existence. If the condition is true (the file does not exist), processing jumps to ERROR1, where the message states that the file does not exist. Then processing skips :EXIT and ends.

Notice that after the COPY and ERASE commands, execution also jumps to :EXIT. The reason is simple. If the file did not jump to :EXIT, MS-DOS would display the "file does not exist" message. Displaying an error message when no error has occurred is not just poor technique, the display is disruptive to the user.

You can modify the batch file again to get rid of the potential for disaster of mistyping or omitting the directory name. In that case, the file is not copied but the old file is erased. One more IF command, an ECHO, and another GOTO handle the problem.

```
ECHO OFF
CLS
IF NOT EXIST C:\%1 GOTO ERROR1
COPY C:\%1 C:\%2 /V
IF NOT EXIST C:\%2\%1 GOTO ERROR2
ERASE C:\%1
GOTO EXIT
:ERROR1
ECHO The file (%1) does not exist...
GOTO EXIT
:ERROR2
ECHO The copy of C:\%1 to C:\%2 was
unsuccessful!
ECHO C:\%1 was not erased.
:EXIT
```

This version tests whether the new file exists and is copied successfully. You combine C:\ with %1, the file name, and %2, the subdirectory that will hold the copied file. The result is a complete file name (C:\%2\%1), which is used in the test for existence. If the file exists, the COPY command was probably successful. If, however, anything is wrong, the batch file does not erase the original. This line is the safety play, using the approach of doing nothing destructive in case something might have gone wrong. When creating batch files, use the approach that everything must be right before destroying any files.

Example 2. Checking Strings

This section presents a practical example that illustrates the string-comparison option of IF. The example creates a special batch file called FORMAT.BAT to prevent accidentally reformatting your hard disk. Suppose that you simply typed the following at the C prompt:

```
FORMAT
```

Because you did not specify the disk drive to format, MS-DOS pre-V3.2 used the default disk—in this case C:, the hard disk drive.

To take some simple action to ensure that an accident like this would not happen easily, you can hide, or disguise, the FORMAT.COM program. For instance, you can rename it XFORMAT.COM (or any other name) with the following command:

```
REN FORMAT.COM  XFORMAT.COM
```

Now, if someone blithely types FORMAT, nothing drastic happens because no such program file exists on the hard disk.

Now create the following batch file and call it FORMAT.BAT:

```
ECHO OFF
IF %1. == . GOTO :NONE
IF %1 == C: GOTO :NOCAN
IF %1 == c: GOTO :NOCAN
```

```
XFORMAT   %1
GOTO END
:NONE ECHO You did not specify the drive
ECHO (B:), e.g. FORMAT B:
ECHO Please try the command again.
:NOCAN
ECHO You don't really mean to do that—
ECHO format the C drive—do you?
:END
```

In this command, the IF subcommand is used to test repeatedly for the equivalence of two strings. Remember that strings are defined as sets of arbitrary (any) characters of arbitrary (any) length. For example, each command line parameter is a string. When comparing two strings, MS-DOS simply compares two sets of characters.

With the renamed file and batch file in place, typing FORMAT b: causes MS-DOS to use the batch file, not FORMAT.COM. FORMAT.COM is now named XFORMAT.COM. MS-DOS substitutes b: for %1. The three IF lines become the following lines:

```
IF b:. == . GOTO :NONE
IF b: == C: GOTO :NOCAN
IF b: == c: GOTO :NOCAN
```

Each IF test executes, finding that b: is not the same as ., C:, or c:. All three tests fail, and MS-DOS drops to the command to execute FORMAT under its new name with the given drive name.

If, for any reason, someone explicitly attempts to format the C drive, line 3 traps the command FORMAT C:. Processing jumps to the label NOCAN, gives the message, and does not format the disk.

Notice the fourth line. MS-DOS is literal in comparing strings. Capital C is not the same as lowercase c. Line 4 handles the difference by repeating the test with a lowercase c. Remember that in matching strings MS-DOS does see a difference between the cases of characters. If you want to test for both uppercase and lowercase letters, you must test for both cases.

Line 2 of this batch file handles the core problem—not using any parameters. The line is less complex than you might expect. You might think that the following line would also work.

    IF %1 == GOTO NOCAN

You may think that the missing second string would designate an empty string, a string with no characters in it. However, MS-DOS substitutes exactly what it "sees" for each parameter. By giving no additional parameters to the batch file, you would get these results:

    IF == GOTO NOCAN

In other words, MS-DOS substitutes nothing for something. MS-DOS is ungracious about comparing nothing to anything and gives a very explanatory Syntax error and pops out of the batch file.

To solve the problem, MS-DOS must see something. A period was used in the batch file. When executing line 2 with no parameters, the line becomes the following:

    IF . == . GOTO NONE

The condition is true, and the program jumps to the message about needing a disk drive name.

The FORMAT.BAT file works for users of MS-DOS V3.1 and earlier versions. MS-DOS V3.2 or V3.3 added some safety features to the FORMAT command: you must enter a drive letter with the command, and you must type the volume label to reformat a hard drive. Thus, the FORMAT.BAT may be unnecessary for V3.2 and V3.3 users.

You can create a similar batch file to protect yourself from catastrophes resulting from improper use of the RECOVER command. You can use MS-DOS RECOVER to salvage as much data as MS-DOS can save from a damaged file or disk. But used improperly, it is as lethal as FORMAT when it is used wrong.

The first step is to rename RECOVER.COM with a name such as XRECOVER.COM. Then write the batch file, which is named RECOVER.BAT:

```
ECHO OFF
IF %1. == . GOTO :NONE
IF %1 == C: GOTO :NOCAN
IF %1 = c: GOTO :NOCAN
XRECOVER %1
GOTO END
:NONE
ECHO You did not specify a drive & file(s),
ECHO e.g., RECOVER B:*.DOC
ECHO If you don't specify a file or files,
ECHO ALL files will be
ECHO recovered and it
ECHO will take you hours to reconstruct them.
:NOCAN
ECHO You have asked the computer to recover
ECHO every file on the hard drive. This is
ECHO almost the same as re-formatting the hard
ECHO drive; it will destroy your files.
ECHO Check with a knowledgeable advisor.
:END
```

Note that this batch file does not prevent a global recovery of files on a floppy diskette. You can change this file to work for a floppy diskette, by adding four lines identical to lines 3 and 4, substituting upper- and lowercase A: and B: for the C:. With the floppy diskette version of the batch file, you can recover any file or files listed (B: will not be equal to B:*.doc), without global recovery.

=PAUSE

Batch Subcommand

Purpose

Suspends batch-file processing until a key is pressed, and optionally displays a user's message

Syntax

PAUSE *message*

message is a string of up to 121 characters.

Rules

1. The *message*, a series of up to 121 characters, must be on the batch-file line with the word PAUSE.

2. When MS-DOS encounters a PAUSE subcommand in a batch file, MS-DOS displays the optional *message* if ECHO is on. If ECHO is off, MS-DOS does not display the optional *message*.

3. Regardless of ECHO's setting, MS-DOS displays the message:

   ```
   Strike a key when ready . . .
   ```

4. MS-DOS suspends the processing of the batch file until you press any key. Afterward, MS-DOS continues processing the batch file's lines. To end a batch file's processing, press Ctrl-Break or Ctrl-C.

Examples

Example 1. Because the `Strike any key when ready. . .` message of PAUSE always shows on-screen, you can phrase your batch-file message to take advantage of this line. For example, you can use these lines:

```
ECHO OFF
CLS
```

```
ECHO Place the proper disk into drive A,
ECHO and when the message appears,
ECHO press Enter to continue
ECHO or press Ctrl-Break
ECHO and then Y to stop the file.
PAUSE
```

This set of lines yields the following screen:

```
Place the proper disk into drive A,
and when the message appears,
press Enter to continue
or press Ctrl-Break
and then Y to stop the file.
Strike a key when ready . . .
```

Example 2. You can rephrase your message as follows:

```
ECHO OFF
CLS
ECHO Place the proper disk into drive A.
ECHO If the disk is not available,
ECHO press Ctrl-Break and then Y
ECHO to stop the file, or
ECHO ......................
ECHO [hard space]
PAUSE
```

This set of lines displays the following message:

```
Place the proper disk into drive A.
If the disk is not available,
press Ctrl-Break and then Y
to stop the file, or
. . . . . . . . . . . . . . . . . .
Strike a key when ready...
```

Adding two lines to this batch file before the pause command makes it much cleaner on-screen:

```
ECHO ......................
ECHO hard space
```

The first line draws a dotted line to separate the message you create with ECHO commands in the batch file from the message that the PAUSE command gives.

The second line is created by typing **ECHO**, pressing the space bar to skip a space, and then holding down the ALT key while you type **255** at the numeric keypad. You see the cursor move one space to the right when this hard space is added. This is a legitimate ECHO command. Only a blank line appears because ASCII 255 is a space.

REM

Batch Subcommand

Purpose
Displays a message within the batch file

Syntax
REM *message*

message is a string of up to 123 characters.

Rules

1. REM must be the last batch-file command on the line when you use REM with the IF or FOR..IN..DO subcommands.

2. The optional *message* can contain up to 123 characters and must immediately follow the word REM.

3. When MS-DOS encounters a REM subcommand in a batch file, MS-DOS displays the *message* if ECHO is on. If ECHO is off, MS-DOS does not display the *message*.

4. The difference between **ECHO** *message* and **REM**
    message is that with ECHO, the message is always
    displayed. IF ECHO is off, the message with REM
    is not displayed.

Example

This example shows the beginning of a sample batch file
with REM commands:

    REM To run this program, make sure
    REM the disk containing BASICA is in
    REM drive A and the disk labeled CONTRACTS
    REM is in drive B.
    REM . . . .
    REM (If you need to exit at this time,
    REM hold down the REM Ctrl key and
    REM press the Break key. When the system
    REM asks you whether you want to
    REM "Terminate batch job (Y/N)?"
    REM press Y. The batch file will stop.)

When this batch file runs, MS-DOS displays the word
REM followed by each remark line on-screen. Nothing
on the line is "executed" by MS-DOS.

Because REM's display of messages is not tidy,
consider using the batch subcommand ECHO.

Both ECHO and REM statements are useful in a batch
file. With ECHO OFF, REM protects comments that
you want to remain in the batch file but do not want to
appear on-screen and ECHO displays messages on-
screen. REM comments can serve as documentation
when you or others want to change the file later, and
ECHO messages can provide on-screen guidance.

With ECHO ON, ECHO statements appear twice and
REM statements once.

SHIFT

Batch Subcommand

Purpose

Shifts one position to the left the parameters given on the command line when the batch file is invoked

Syntax

SHIFT

Rules

1. When you use SHIFT, MS-DOS moves the command line parameters one position to the left.

2. MS-DOS discards the former first parameter (%0).

3. When you write a batch file to execute a command that works in pairs, such as RENAME, include two SHIFT commands instead of one. Each SHIFT command is an executable MS-DOS command, so each one must be placed on its own line.

Examples

Example 1. Using More than 10 Parameters

MS-DOS enables the explicit use of only 10 batch parameters, %0 through %9. However, MS-DOS can be tricked into using more parameters by use of the batch subcommand SHIFT. Placing SHIFT in a batch file moves each command line parameter one position to the left. In other words, parameter 0 (zero) is discarded, old parameter 1 becomes new parameter 0, old parameter 2 becomes new parameter 1, and so on.

SHIFT commonly is used when you are handling an undetermined number of similar parameters. For instance, you can take a file called MOVE.BAT (one that moves files to a predetermined subdirectory) and generalize it so that it can move any number of files.

```
ECHO OFF
CLS
:START
IF NOT EXIST C:\%1 GOTO ERROR1
COPY C:\%1 C:\SUBDIR1 /V
ERASE C:\%1
SHIFT
IF %1. == . GOTO EXIT
GOTO START
GOTO EXIT
:ERROR1
ECHO The file (%1) does not exist...
:EXIT
```

To move any number of files, you can enter a command like the following:

```
MOVE COMP.COM ABACUS.EXE
SLIDE.EXE LINK.EXE ABSCOND.COM
```

MOVE.BAT substitutes the first file (COMP.COM) for %1, processes the file, and shifts the parameters so that the second file (ABACUS.EXE) now becomes %1, and so on.

Example 2. Using SHIFT for repetitive work.

The most frequent use of SHIFT is to do the same work on an unknown number of files, for example, running the Macro Assembler on any set of files. The batch file that does this work looks similar to the MOVE file.

```
ECHO OFF
CLS
:START
IF %1. == . GOTO EXIT
IF NOT EXIST %1 GOTO MISSING
MASM %1;
SHIFT
GOTO START
:MISSING
ECHO %1 does not exist...
```

```
SHIFT
GOTO START
:EXIT
```

ECHO is turned off and the screen cleared. MS-DOS immediately tests for an empty parameter and jumps to the EXIT line if %1 is empty. Processing goes to a warning message if a named file does not exist. Otherwise, MS-DOS invokes the Macro Assembler, MASM .EXE, with the correct arguments. The file then shifts the batch-file parameters one position to the left and loops back to the test for an empty parameter.

If this batch file encounters a wrong name, it informs the user about the error but continues to work on the other files. Nothing is more infuriating than having to retype a complete command line when just one file name is wrong. Because MASM does not alter the original files, the approach for this application is safe and practical.

The DOS Line Editor (EDLIN)

What Is EDLIN?

EDLIN is a *line editor*. A line editor works with text one
line at a time. EDLIN is not as sophisticated as a word-
processing program or other full-screen editors, but it
does allow for quick entry of small programs, such as
batch files and DOS text messages.

Although you can create small files faster with COPY
CON, you can't edit a COPY CON line if you have
already pressed the Enter key. If you plan to do involved
programming or text entry, you should probably use a
good word-processing program.

Use EDLIN To:

Create, edit, and save batch, program, and text files.

Create source files for BASIC, assembly language, or
any programming language.

Create control codes and special graphic characters to be
used in a file.

Before You Use EDLIN

Follow instructions below to start the EDLIN program.
This program explains how to create a file, enter text,
and save the file.

Note that EDLIN is a separate program with its own
commands. EDLIN must be running before you can use
its commands.

Starting EDLIN

Syntax

dc:pathc**EDLIN** d:path**filename.ext**/B

Procedures

1. Type **EDLIN** and press the space bar. Because EDLIN is an external program, you may need to precede the command with a drive name and path.

2. Type the drive name, path, and name of the file to be created or edited. Do not use wild-card characters (* or ?). If EDLIN does not find the file name you type, the message New file is displayed.

3. If you want to use a file that contains an end-of-file character (Ctrl-Z or ^Z), type /**B**.

4. Press Enter.

5. Choose EDLIN commands from the following chart to create or edit files. To start entering the text of a new file, press the **I** key and then press Enter.

6. If you are editing an existing file, you may press **L** to list the file's lines.

7. Select the line number you want to edit and press Enter.

8. Change the displayed text line until the line is correct. You can insert up to 253 characters per line in the text. EDLIN will wrap the line automatically.

9. When you press Enter, the cursor will return to the (*) prompt.

10. To exit EDLIN, use either the **E** command to save and quit or the **Q** command to exit without saving.

EDLIN Commands

Command   *Function*

A   *Appends* when file is too large for memory

C   *Copies* one or more lines in a file

D   *Deletes* one or more lines from a file

E   *Ends* the EDLIN program and saves the file

I   *Inserts* new text lines

L   *Lists* and displays a file's contents

M   *Moves* lines in a file

P   Lists a block of specified lines

Q   *Quits* without saving changes

R   *Replaces* text in the file

S   *Searches* for a specified text string

T   *Transfers* and merges two files

W   *Writes* a specified number of lines to disk

Notes

In EDLIN, the system prompt appears as an asterisk (*).

All EDLIN commands consist of a single letter, but many use options and other parameters.

Line numbers that appear in EDLIN are used for tracking and are not saved in the file. Line numbers can range from 1 to 65,529.

When you edit an existing file with EDLIN, a backup copy with the extension .BAK is created.

When you enter a line number and press Enter in EDLIN, the line to be edited appears. If you press Enter without typing a line number, you can edit the current line.

You can add control characters to a file by pressing Ctrl-V and then typing the character in uppercase letters. To type a Ctrl-Z character, press Ctrl-V and then type Z.

To add Escape (ASCII 27) to a file, press Ctrl-V and then press [.

To enter a special character, hold down the Alt-Shift keys and type on the numeric keypad the ASCII code of the graphics character you want. This procedure will work, providing that you have installed ANSI.SYS in your CONFIG.SYS file.

You can cancel editing by pressing Enter when the cursor is in the first position of the current line.

To cancel a command within EDLIN, press Ctrl-C or Ctrl- Break.

Caution

When you edit, be sure that the cursor is at the beginning or end of the line before you press Enter. If the cursor is elsewhere, you may erase whole or partial lines.

A (Append Lines)

EDLIN Subcommand

Purpose

Appends the number of lines you specify to the end of the lines currently in memory. You only use EDLIN's

Append command when the file you are editing is too
large to fit into memory.

Procedures

1. If you have added or changed any lines in the file
   being edited, use the W command to write the
   changes to disk before you use the Append
   command.

2. You can then enter the number of lines you want to
   append to the end of memory.

3. Type A and press Enter to return to the * prompt.

4. Repeat Procedures 1 through 3 until you see the
   message

   ```
   End of input file
   ```

   When this message appears, all lines have been read
   into memory.

Notes

If the number of lines to append with the A command is
not specified, all remaining lines are appended until
available memory is 75% full.

Caution

If you do not use use the W (Write) command before
using APPEND, you can lose your previous editing
corrections.

C (Copy Lines)

EDLIN Subcommand

Purpose

Copies one or more lines from the file to the line number
you specify

Syntax

line,*line*,**line**,*count*C

Procedures

1. If you like, type the line number that marks the first line in the block (or group of lines). This line is where the copying will begin.

2. Type a comma, the number of the line that ends the block, another comma, and the line number where the block will be copied. If you want to copy the block more than once, type another comma and the number of copies you want.

3. Type **C** and press Enter. The cursor will return to the * prompt.

Notes

Text blocks are copied to the area before the line number you specify. For example, type **5,10,15C** to copy six lines of text (line 5 to line 10) on line 15. The copied lines will be placed before line 15, and the original line 15 will now be renumbered line 21.

If the first or second parameter is missing, the default is the current line. When you make the copy, only the current line will be copied to the designated line number.

If only one line is being copied, ignore the second parameter, but leave the commas in place. For instance, **2,,4C** copies line 2 to line 4.

Caution

Do not overlap line numbers. For example, **2,7,5C** would result in an error because lines 2 to 7 overlap line number 5.

D (Delete Lines)

EDLIN Subcommand

Purpose

Deletes one or more lines from the file to the line number you specify

Syntax

> *line,line*D

Procedures

1. Enter the line number to be deleted. If you are going to delete a range of line numbers, this line will be the first one within the block to be deleted.

2. If you are going to delete more than one line, type a comma (,) followed by the line number that ends the block to be deleted. The block to be deleted will consist of all lines ranging from the first parameter entered in Step 1 to and including the line number entered in this step.

3. Type D and press Enter to delete the lines and return the cursor to the * prompt.

Notes

Before you delete lines, make sure of your line numbers by using the List command, L, before you delete.

The line following the deleted range becomes the current line. The current line and the lines that follow are then renumbered.

If you typed 4,10D to delete lines 4 through 10 of a 20-line program, you would be left with a 13-line program. The original line 11 becomes line 4. What was line 20 is now line 13. The current line is now line 4.

Omit the second parameter if you want to delete just one line.

To delete the current line, simply press **D** and then press
Enter. The following line then becomes the current line.

E (Exit)

EDLIN Subcommand

Purpose

Exits EDLIN and saves the file

Procedures

1. Type **E**.

2. Press Enter. The cursor will return to the system
   prompt.

Notes

Before you exit, use CHKDSK to determine if you have
enough space on your disk to save the original file and a
backup copy.

To keep a backup file intact, rename it before you edit
the original file.

When you save a file, a carriage return and end-of-file
character, Ctrl-Z, are automatically provided.

Cautions

DOS does not make a backup file when you are creating
a new file. Backup files are created only if you are
editing an existing file.

If there is insufficient space on the disk to save the files,
the original file remains intact as though never edited.
The portion that was saved is given the root name of the
file and the extension .$$$.

I (Insert Lines)

EDLIN Subcommand

Purpose

Adds text to a newly-created file and inserts new lines of text between lines or at the end of existing files

Syntax

*line*I

Procedures

1. Type the line number where you want to begin inserting new lines. If you do not supply a line number, the insertion begins with the current line. If you are creating a new file, skip this option and go to Step 2, because new files always begin on line 1.

2. Type I and press Enter. The cursor will move to the right of the insert prompt, which includes the line number being inserted, a colon (:), and an asterisk(*).

3. Type the text you want to insert on the line and press Enter.

4. When you finish inserting lines, press Ctrl-C to return to the EDLIN * prompt.

Notes

If you do not specify a line number, the insertion occurs just before the current line.

As the new lines are inserted, the current line and those that follow are renumbered.

To insert lines at the end of the file, use the symbol # as the line number. Insertion begins after the last line number.

You can insert several lines in succession. After you type the first line to insert, press Enter. A new line

number appears for the next line to insert. This process
is repeated each time you press Enter.

Caution

EDLIN's insert command changes line numbers in the
original program, so a previous line number may have
changed. Use the **L** (list) command frequently to be sure
of your place in the program.

L (List Lines)

EDLIN Subcommand

Purpose

Displays one or more lines from the file

Syntax

*line,line***L**

Procedures

1. You can type the number of the line where the
   displayed block is to begin. If you omit this first
   parameter, the List command displays the 11 lines
   that precede the current line and ends with the
   specified line.

2. If you use Step 1, type a comma and the line
   number where the displayed block is to end. If you
   omit the second parameter, the 23 lines that follow
   the specified line will be displayed.

   If you type **L** without parameters, 11 lines before
   the current line, the current line, and 11 lines after
   the current line will be displayed. If the current line
   is less than 11 lines from the beginning of the file,
   lines 1-23 will be displayed.

3. When you press Enter, the cursor returns to the *
   prompt.

Notes

The list command works like the EDLIN **P** (page) command with one exception: the current line does not change as lines are displayed.

If you want to list the lines numbered 12 to 20, type **12,20L**.

You can refer to line numbers from the current line by using the plus (+) or minus (-) sign. If you want to list the next 11 lines after the current line, type **+11L.** To list the 5 lines that precede the current line, type **-5L**.

Use the Pause key or Ctrl-S to stop the screen display from scrolling.

M (Move Lines)

EDLIN Subcommand

Purpose

Moves lines within a file

Syntax

*line,line,*line **M**

Procedures

1. Type the line number of the block's first line, a comma, and the last line number of the block of text to be moved.

2. Type another comma and the number of the line where the block is to move.

3. Type **M** and press Enter to move the designated line(s) and return to the * prompt.

Notes

If you want to move lines 25 through 40 and insert them at line 71, type **25,40,71M**

To move a single line, omit the second parameter. For example, to move line 3 to the position of line 7, type **3,,7M**.

To move the current line to another location, leave the first and second parameters empty and add the number of the line where you want to move the current line. For example, typing **,,3M** moves the current line to line 3.

To move the current line and a designated number of lines to another location, leave the first parameter empty and add a + sign to the second parameter. For example, to move the current line plus the next 7 lines to line 3, type **,+7,3M**

Caution

The third parameter is not optional. Be sure you indicate where the line of text is to be moved.

P (Page)

EDLIN Subcommand

Purpose

Page through a file 23 lines at a time.

Syntax

*line,line***P**

Procedures

1. To display a particular page of text, type the line number that begins the block to be displayed, a comma, and the line number that ends the block to be displayed. If you do not add a number for the second parameter, the next 23 lines will be listed.

2. Type **P** and press Enter to return to the * prompt.

Notes

This command works like EDLIN's **L** (List) command except that the current line is changed. With **P**, the new current line becomes the last line displayed.

Use Ctrl-S or the Pause key to stop the screen display from scrolling.

If you omit the first parameter, Page starts displaying the line after the current line. The listing continues to display 23 consecutive lines at a time until the specified line is reached.

If you omit the second parameter, the 23 lines displayed start at the specified line. For example, if you type **12P**, lines 12 to 35 appear on the screen.

If you type **P** only, the next 23 lines after the current line will be displayed.

If you want to display lines 12 through 20 and make 20 the current line, type **12,20P**

To list 23 lines starting at line 5, type **5P**

Q (Quit)

EDLIN Subcommand

Purpose

Quits EDLIN without saving the file

Procedures

1. Press **Q**. EDLIN verifies whether you want to terminate the editing program without saving the file by prompting Abort edit (Y/N)? Press **Y** to abort editing or **N** to continue editing the file.

2. Press Enter. The cursor will return to the system prompt.

Notes

Before you quit EDLIN, determine whether you want to exit the editing session and lose the file in memory.

R (Replace text)

EDLIN Subcommand

Purpose

Replaces characters or deletes text

Syntax

line,line ?**R**text<**F6**>*text*

Procedures

1. Type the line number where text replacement is to begin. If you are changing only one line, enter that line number as the first parameter. If you omit this parameter, DOS will change the current line.

2. Type a comma and the line number at the end of the block where text replacement will occur.

3. If you want to respond line by line whether a line should be changed, press ?.

4. Type **R**

5. If you want DOS to search for a text string to be replaced, type the text string.

6. If you intend to delete the text, instead of replacing it, skip Step 5.

7. Press Enter to make the replacement and return to the * prompt.

Notes

If you do not specify the first-line parameter, the search to replace begins with the line following the current line.

If you do not specify the second-line parameter, replacement ends with the current line.

If you specify no line parameters at all, the search to replace begins at the line following the current line and continues until it finds either the last line in memory or the end of the file.

The last line changed becomes the default or current line.

Cautions

If you do not specify a replacement text string, all occurrences of the first string will be deleted from the lines you have specified.

If both text strings are unspecified, then EDLIN uses the values specified in the last search or replace command.

S (Search)

EDLIN Subcommand

Purpose

Searches for a sequence of characters

Syntax

line,line ?S*text*

Procedures

1. Type the line number where text searching is to start, a comma, and the line number of the end of the block where text searching will end.

2. Press the space bar.

3. Type ? if you want DOS to query whether to stop searching and make the last displayed line the current default line.

4. Type S.

5. Type the text string you want to search for.

6. Press Enter to search and return the cursor to the * prompt.

Notes

If you do not specify the first line, the search begins with the line following the current line.

If you do not specify the second line, the search continues to the end of the file or the last line in memory.

If you don't use the ? parameter, the search will stop on the first occurrence of the text string.

If you do not specify line parameters, the search begins at the line following the current line and continues to the last line in memory or the end of the file.

The message Not found appears when DOS cannot find the text string within the specified lines.

Caution

Search strings are case sensitive. For example, if you search for the word capital, you will not locate the words Capital or CAPITAL.

T (Transfer)

EDLIN Subcommand

Purpose

Transfers or merges the contents of files

Syntax

*line*T*d*:**filename**

Procedures

1. Type the line number where the merged file contents are to be inserted. If you do not specify a line number, the current default line is used.

2. Type T.

3. Type the drive name, such as A:, B:, and so on. You cannot designate a path.

4. Type the name of the file to be merged with the file being edited.

5. Press Enter to merge and return the cursor to the * prompt.

Notes

Before you transfer files, check to see whether the file being merged is an ASCII file. Use DOS's TYPE command to see if the file is readable.

The contents of the merged file are inserted at the beginning of the current line or the line number you specify.

For example, assume that you are editing the following file:

```
1:  *__Line  1
2:  Line  2
3:  Line  3
```

If you enter the command 2Tnewfile, a file named NEWFILE will be inserted at the beginning of the specified line and the edited file might look like this:

```
1:  Line  1
2:  * The  new  file  shows  up  here,  and
3:  continues  until  the  entire  file  has
4:  been   inserted.
```

```
5:  Line  2
6:  Line  3
```

Also notice that the current line has changed from 1 to 2.

W (Write)

EDLIN Subcommand

Purpose

Writes and saves lines when file being edited is too large
to fit in memory

Syntax

*n*W

Procedures

1. Type the number of lines you want to write to the
   end of memory.

2. Type W and press Enter to return to the * prompt.

3. Repeat the first two Procedures until you see the
   message End of input file. When this
   message appears, all lines have been read into
   memory.

Notes

Use the W command whenever you have made changes
to a file that was not fully loaded into memory.

Use the W command before appending new lines to the
file being edited.

If you fail to use the W command before you use the A
(Append) command, you can lose all your edited text.

When you do not specify the number of lines in the W
command, the lines beginning at line 1 are saved to the
disk until available memory is 25% full.

MS-DOS Messages

MS-DOS messages fall into two groups; *general* MS-DOS messages and MS-DOS *device error* messages. The larger group, general MS-DOS messages, is listed first, followed by the device error messages.

The actual wordings of error messages for your implementation and version of MS-DOS may differ from those shown here. Sometimes the differences may be as slight as punctuation and capitalization. Other times, the entire content of the message may differ. If you see a message that you cannot locate in this guide, refer to your computer's MS-DOS manual.

General MS-DOS Messages

The following messages may appear when you are starting MS-DOS or using your computer. Messages that usually appear when you are starting MS-DOS are marked (start-up). Most start-up errors mean that MS-DOS did not start and that you must reboot the system. Most of the other error messages mean that MS-DOS terminated (aborted) the program and returned to the system prompt (A>). The messages are listed in alphabetical order for easy reference.

Bad command or filename

ERROR: The name you entered is not valid for invoking a command, program, or batch file. The most frequent causes are the following: (1) you misspelled a name; (2) you omitted a needed disk drive or path name; or (3) you gave the parameters without the command name, such as typing **myfile** instead of **ws myfile** (omitting the ws for WordStar).

Check the spelling on the command line. Make sure that the command, program, or batch file is in the location specified (disk drive and directory path). Then try the command again.

Bad or missing Command Interpreter

ERROR (start-up): MS-DOS cannot find the command interpreter, COMMAND.COM. MS-DOS does not start.

If you are starting MS-DOS, this message means that COMMAND.COM is not on the boot disk or that a version of COMMAND.COM from a previous MS-DOS is on the disk. If you have used the SHELL directive of CONFIG.SYS, the message means that it is improperly phrased or that COMMAND.COM is not where you specified. Place in the floppy disk drive another diskette that contains the operating system and then reset the system. After MS-DOS has started, copy COMMAND.COM to the original start-up disk so that you can boot from that disk.

If resetting the system does not solve your problem, use a copy of your MS-DOS master diskette to restart the computer. Copy COMMAND.COM from this diskette to the offending disk.

Bad or missing filename

WARNING (start-up): MS-DOS was requested to load a device driver that could not be located, an error occurred when the device driver was loaded, or a break address for the device driver was out of bounds for the size of RAM memory being used in the computer. MS-DOS will continue its boot but will not use the device driver filename.

If MS-DOS loads, check your CONFIG.SYS file for the line DEVICE=filename. Make sure that the line is spelled correctly and that the device driver is where you specified. If this line is correct, reboot the system. If the message appears again, copy the file from its original diskette to the boot diskette and try booting MS-DOS again. If the error persists, contact the dealer or publisher that sold you the driver, because the device driver is bad.

Batch file missing

ERROR: MS-DOS could not find the batch file it was
processing. The batch file may have been erased or
renamed. For MS-DOS V3.0 only, the diskette
containing the batch file may have been changed.
MS-DOS aborts the processing of the batch file.

If you are using MS-DOS V3.0 and you changed the
diskette containing the batch file, restart the batch file
and do not change the diskette. You may need to edit the
batch file so that you will not need to change diskettes.

If you renamed the batch file, rename it again, using the
original name. If required, edit the batch file to ensure
that the file name does not get changed again.

If the file was erased, re-create the batch file from its
backup file if possible. Edit the file to ensure that the
batch file does not erase itself.

Cannot load COMMAND, system halted

ERROR: MS-DOS attempted to reload
COMMAND.COM, but the area where MS-DOS keeps
track of available and used memory was destroyed, or
the command processor was not found in the directory
specified by the COMSPEC= entry. The system halts.

This message indicates either that COMMAND.COM
has been erased from the disk and directory you used
when starting MS-DOS, or that the COMSPEC= entry
in the environment has been changed. Restart MS-DOS.
If it does not start, the copy of COMMAND.COM has
been erased. Restart MS-DOS from the original master
diskettes and copy COMMAND.COM to your other
disk.

Cannot start COMMAND, exiting

ERROR: MS-DOS was directed to load an additional
copy of COMMAND.COM, but could not. Either your

CONFIG.SYS FILES= command is set too low, or you
do not have enough free memory for another copy of
COMMAND.COM.

If your system has 256K or more and FILES is less than
10, edit the CONFIG.SYS file on your start-up diskette
and use FILES = 15 or FILES = 20, then reboot.

If the problem occurs again, you do not have enough
memory in your computer or you have too many
resident or background programs competing for memory
space. Restart MS-DOS again and do not load any
resident or background programs you do not need. If
necessary, eliminate unneeded device drivers or RAM
disk software. Another alternative is to increase the
amount of RAM memory in your system.

Configuration too large

ERROR (start-up): MS-DOS could not load itself
because you specified too many FILES or BUFFERS in
your CONFIG.SYS file. This problem should occur only
on 128K or 192K systems.

Restart MS-DOS with a different diskette and edit the
CONFIG.SYS file on your boot diskette, lowering the
number of FILES and/or BUFFERS. Restart MS-DOS
with the edited diskette. Another alternative is to
increase the RAM memory in your system.

Current drive is no longer valid

WARNING: You have set the system prompt to
PROMPT $p. At the system level, MS-DOS attempted
to read the current directory for the disk drive and found
the drive no longer valid.

If the current disk drive is set for a floppy disk, this
warning appears when you do not have a diskette in the
disk drive. MS-DOS reports a Drive not ready
error. You give the F command to fail (which is the

same as A for abort) or the I command to ignore the error. Then insert a floppy diskette into the disk drive.

The invalid drive error also can happen if you have a current networked or SUBST disk drive that has been deleted or disconnected. Simply change the current disk to a valid disk drive.

Disk boot failure

ERROR (start-up): An error occurred when MS-DOS tried to load itself into memory. The diskette contained IO.SYS and MSDOS.SYS, but one of the two files could not be loaded. MS-DOS did not boot.

Try starting MS-DOS from the diskette again. If the error recurs, try booting MS-DOS from diskette you know is good, such as a copy of your MS-DOS master diskette. If this action fails, you have a hardware disk drive problem. Contact your local dealer.

Divide overflow

ERROR: A program attempted to divide by zero. MS-DOS aborts the program. Either the program was incorrectly entered, or it has a logic flaw. With well-written programs, this error should never occur. If you wrote the program, correct the error and try the program again. If you purchased the program, report the problem to the dealer or publisher.

This message can also appear when you are attempting to format a RAM disk. Make sure that you are formatting the correct disk and try again.

Error in COUNTRY command

WARNING (start-up): The COUNTRY directive in CONFIG.SYS is either improperly phrased or has an incorrect country code or code page number. MS-DOS continues its start-up but uses the default information for the COUNTRY directive.

After MS-DOS has started, check the COUNTRY line in your CONFIG.SYS file. Ensure that the directive is correctly phrased (using commas between country code, code page, and COUNTRY.SYS file) and that any given information is correct. If you detect an error in the line, edit the line, save the file, and restart MS- DOS.

If you do not find an error, restart MS-DOS. If the same message appears, edit your CONFIG.SYS file. Reenter the COUNTRY directive and delete the old COUNTRY line. The old line may contain some nonsense characters that MS-DOS can see but are not apparent to your text editing program.

Error in EXE file

ERROR: MS-DOS detected an error while attempting to load a program stored in an .EXE file. The problem is in the relocation information MS-DOS needs to load the program. This problem can occur if the .EXE file has been altered in any way.

Restart MS-DOS and try the program again, this time using a backup copy of the program. If the message reappears, the program is flawed. If you are using a purchased program, contact the dealer or publisher. If you wrote the program, use LINK to produce another copy of the program.

Error loading operating system

ERROR (start-up): A disk error occurred while MS-DOS was loading itself from the hard disk. MS-DOS does not boot.

Restart the computer. If the error occurs after several tries, restart MS-DOS from the floppy disk drive. If the hard disk does not respond (that is, you cannot run DIR or CHKDSK without getting an error), you have a problem with the hard disk. Contact your local dealer. If the hard disk does respond, use the SYS command to put another copy of MS-DOS onto your hard disk. You may need to copy COMMAND.COM to the hard disk also.

EXEC failure

ERROR: MS-DOS encountered an error while reading a command or program from the disk, or the CONFIG.SYS FILES= command has too low a value.

Increase the number of FILES in the CONFIG.SYS file of your start-up disk to 15 or 20, then restart MS-DOS. If the error recurs, you may have a problem with the disk. Use a backup copy of the program and try again. If the backup copy works, copy it over the offending copy.

If an error occurs in the copying process, you have a flawed diskette or hard disk. If the problem is a diskette, copy the files from the flawed diskette to another diskette and reformat or retire the original diskette. If the problem is the hard disk, immediately back up your files and run RECOVER on the offending file. If the problem persists, your hard disk may have a hardware failure.

File allocation table bad, drive d Abort, Retry, Fail?

WARNING: MS-DOS encountered a problem in the File Allocation Table (FAT) of the disk in drive d. Enter R for Retry several times. If this does not solve the problem, use A for Abort.

If you are using a diskette, attempt to copy all the files to another diskette and then reformat or retire the original diskette. If you are using a hard disk, back up all files on the disk and reformat the hard disk. The disk is unusable until reformatted.

File creation error

ERROR: A program or MS-DOS attempted to add a new file to the directory or replace an existing file, but failed.

If the file already exists, use the ATTRIB command to check whether the file is marked as read-only. If the read-only flag is set and you want to change or erase the file, use ATTRIB to remove the read-only flag and then try again.

If the problem is not a read-only flag, run CHKDSK without the /F switch to determine whether the directory is full, the disk is full, or some other problem exists with the disk.

File not found

ERROR: MS-DOS could not find the file you specified. The file is not on the correct diskette or in the correct directory; or you misspelled the disk drive name, path name, or file name. Check these possibilities and try the command again.

Filename device driver cannot be initialized

WARNING (start-up): In CONFIG.SYS, either the parameters in the device driver filename are incorrect, or the DEVICE line is in error. Check for incorrect parameters, and check for phrasing errors in the DEVICE line. Edit the DEVICE line in the CONFIG.SYS file, save the file, and restart MS-DOS.

Incorrect MS-DOS version

ERROR: The copy of the file holding the command you just entered is from a different version of MS-DOS.

Get a copy of the command from the correct version of
MS-DOS (usually from your copy of the MS-DOS
master diskette) and try the command again. If the disk
or diskette you are using has been updated to hold new
versions of the MS-DOS programs, copy those versions
over the old ones.

Insert disk with \COMMAND.COM in drive d and strike any key when ready

INFORMATIONAL and WARNING: MS-DOS needed
to reload COMMAND.COM but could not find it on the
start-up disk.

If you are using diskettes, probably the diskette in drive
A: has been changed. Place a diskette holding a good
copy of COMMAND.COM in drive A: and press a key.

Insert disk with batch file and strike any key when ready

INFORMATIONAL: MS-DOS is attempting to execute
the next command from a batch file, but the diskette
holding the batch file was removed from the disk drive.
This message occurs for MS-DOS V3.1. MS-DOS V3.0
gives a fatal error when the diskette is changed.

Put the diskette holding the batch file into the disk drive
and press a key to continue.

Insert diskette for drive d and strike any key when ready

INFORMATIONAL: On a system with one floppy disk
drive, you or one of your programs specified the tandem
disk drive d (A or B). This drive is different from the
current disk drive.

If the correct diskette is in the disk drive, press a key.
Otherwise, put the correct diskette into the floppy disk
drive and then press a key.

Insufficient disk space

WARNING or ERROR: The disk does not have enough
free space to hold the file being written. All MS-DOS
programs terminate when this problem occurs, but some
non-DOS programs continue.

If you think that the disk has enough room to hold this
file, run CHKDSK to see whether the disk or diskette
has a problem. Sometimes when you terminate programs
early by pressing Ctrl-Break, MS-DOS is not allowed to
do the necessary clean-up work. When this happens,
disk space is temporarily trapped. CHKDSK can "free"
these areas.

If you simply have run out of disk space, free some disk
space or use a different diskette or hard disk. Try the
command again.

Insufficient memory

ERROR: The computer does not have enough free RAM
memory to execute the program or command.

If you loaded a resident program like PRINT,
GRAPHICS, SideKick, or ProKey, restart MS-DOS and
try the command before loading any resident program. If
this method fails, remove any unneeded device driver or
RAM-disk software from the CONFIG.SYS file and
restart MS-DOS again. If this action fails, your
computer does not have enough memory for this
command. You must increase your RAM memory to run
the command.

Intermediate file error during pipe

ERROR: MS-DOS is unable to create or write to one or both of the intermediate files it uses when piping (|) information between programs. The disk or root directory is full, or MS-DOS cannot locate the files. The most frequent cause is running out of disk space.

Run the DIR command on the root directory of the current disk drive. Make sure that you have enough free space and enough room in the root directory for two additional files. If you do not have enough room, create room on the disk by deleting, or copying and deleting, files. You may also copy the necessary files to a different diskette with sufficient room.

One possibility is that a program is deleting files, including the temporary files MS-DOS uses. If this is the case, you should correct the program, contact the dealer or program publisher, or avoid using the program with piping.

Internal stack overflow
System halted

ERROR: Your programs and MS-DOS have exhausted the stack, the memory space that is reserved for temporary use. This problem is usually caused by a rapid succession of hardware devices demanding attention (interrupts). If you want to prevent this error from occurring at all, add the STACKS directive to your CONFIG.SYS file. If the directive is already in your CONFIG.SYS file, then increase the number of stacks specified.

Invalid COMMAND.COM in drive d

WARNING: MS-DOS tried to reload COMMAND. COM from the disk in drive d and found that the file was of a different version of MS-DOS. You will see a message instructing you to insert a diskette with the correct

version and press a key. Follow the directions for
that message.

If you frequently use the diskette that was originally in
the disk drive, copy the correct version of
COMMAND.COM to that diskette.

Invalid COUNTRY code or code page

WARNING (start-up): Either the COUNTRY code
number or the code page number given to the
COUNTRY directive in the CONFIG.SYS file is
incorrect or incompatible. MS-DOS ignores the
COUNTRY directive and continues to start.

Check the COUNTRY directive in your CONFIG.SYS
file. Ensure that the correct and compatible country code
and code page numbers are specified. If you detect an
error, edit and save the file, and restart MS-DOS.

Invalid COMMAND.COM, system halted

ERROR: MS-DOS could not find COMMAND.COM
on the hard disk. MS-DOS halts and must be restarted.

COMMAND.COM may have been erased, or the
COMSPEC= setting in the environment may have been
changed. Restart the computer from the hard disk. If you
see a message indicating that COMMAND.COM is
missing, that file was erased. Restart MS-DOS from a
diskette and recopy COMMAND.COM to the root
directory of the hard disk or to wherever your SHELL
command directs, if you have used this command in
your CONFIG.SYS file.

If you restart MS-DOS and this message appears later, a
program or batch file is erasing COMMAND.COM or is
altering the COMSPEC= parameter. If a batch file is
erasing COMMAND.COM, edit the batch file. If a
program is erasing COMMAND.COM, contact the
dealer or publisher that sold you the program. If

COMSPEC= is being altered, either edit the offending batch file or program, or place COMMAND.COM in the subdirectory your program or batch file expects.

Invalid directory

ERROR: One of the following errors occurred: (1) you specified a directory name that does not exist; (2) you misspelled the directory name; (3) the directory path is on a different disk; (4) you forgot to give the path character (\) at the beginning of the name; or (5) you did not separate the directory names with the path character. Check your directory names, ensure that the directories do exist, and try the command again.

Invalid disk change

WARNING: The diskette in the 720K, 1.2M, or 1.44M disk drive was changed while a program had open files to be written to the diskette. You will see the message Abort, Retry, Fail. Place the correct diskette in the disk drive and type R for Retry.

Invalid drive in search path

WARNING: One specification you gave to the PATH command has an invalid disk drive name, or a named disk drive is nonexistent or hidden temporarily by a SUBST or JOIN command.

Use PATH to check the paths you instructed MS-DOS to search. If you gave a nonexistent disk drive name, use the PATH command again and enter the correct search paths. If the problem is temporary because of a SUBST or JOIN command, you can again use PATH to enter the paths, but leave out or correct the wrong entry. Or you can just ignore the warning message.

Invalid drive specification

ERROR: This message occurs if (1) you entered the name

of an invalid or nonexistent disk drive as a parameter to
a command; (2) you have given the same disk drive for
the source and destination, which is not permitted for the
command; or (3) by not giving a parameter, you have
defaulted to the same source and destination disk drive.

Remember that certain MS-DOS commands (such as
SUBST and JOIN) temporarily hide disk drive names
while the command is in effect. Check the disk drive
names. If the command is objecting to a missing
parameter and defaulting to the wrong disk drive,
explicitly name the correct disk drive.

Invalid drive specification
Specified drive does not exist,
or is non-removable

ERROR: One of the following errors occurred: (1) you
gave the name of a nonexistent disk drive; (2) you
named the hard disk drive when using commands for
diskettes only; (3) you did not give a disk drive name
and defaulted to the hard disk when using commands for
diskettes only; or (4) you named or defaulted to a RAM-
disk drive when using commands for a "real" floppy
diskette only.

Remember that certain MS-DOS commands (such as
SUBST and JOIN) temporarily hide disk drive names
while the command is in effect. Check the disk drive
name you gave and try the command again.

Invalid environment size specified

WARNING: You have given the SHELL directive in
CONFIG.SYS. The environment-size switch (/E:size)
contains either nonnumeric characters or a number that
is less than 160 or greater than 32768.

If you are using the SHELL /E:size switch of MS-DOS
V3.1, size is the number of 16-byte memory blocks, not
the number of bytes.

Check the form of your CONFIG.SYS SHELL
directive; the form needs to be exact. There must be a
colon between /E and *size*; there must not be a comma
or space between or within the /E: and the *size*
characters; and the number in *size* should be greater than
or equal to 160, but less than or equal to 32768.

Invalid number of parameters

ERROR: You have given either too few or too many
parameters to a command. One of the following errors
occurred: (1) you omitted required information; (2) you
forgot a colon immediately after the disk drive name;
(3) you put a space in the wrong place or omitted a
needed space; or (4) you forgot to place a slash (/) in
front of a switch.

Invalid parameter
Incorrect parameter

ERROR: At least one parameter you entered for the
command is not valid. One of the following occurred:
(1) you omitted required information; (2) you forgot a
colon immediately after the disk drive name; (3) you put
a space in the wrong place or omitted a needed space;
(4) you forgot to place a slash (/) in front of a switch; or
(5) you used a switch the command does not recognize.

Invalid partition table

ERROR (start-up): While you were attempting to start
MS-DOS from the hard disk, MS-DOS detected a
problem in the hard disk's partition information.

Restart MS-DOS from a diskette. Back up all files from
the hard disk if possible. Run FDISK to correct the
problem. If you change the partition information, you
must reformat the hard disk and restore all its files.

Invalid path

ERROR: One of the following errors has occurred to a path name you have entered: (1) the path name contains illegal characters; (2) the name has more than 63 characters; or (3) one of the directory names within the path is misspelled or does not exist.

Check the spelling of the path name. If needed, do a DIR of the disk and ensure that the directory you have specified does exist and that you have the correct path name. Be sure that the path name contains 63 characters or less. If necessary, change the current directory to a directory "closer" to the file and shorten the path name.

Invalid STACK parameter

WARNING (start-up): One of the following errors has occurred to the STACKS directive in your CONFIG.SYS file: (1) a comma is missing between the number of stacks and the size of the stack; (2) the number of stack frames is not in the range of 8 to 64, (3) the stack size is not in the range of 32 to 512, (4) you have omitted either the number of stack frames or the stack size, or (5) either the stack frame or the stack size (but not both) is 0. MS-DOS continues to start but ignores the STACKS directive.

Check the STACKS directive in your CONFIG.SYS file. Edit and save the file, and restart MS-DOS.

Invalid switch character

WARNING: You have used VDISK.SYS in your CONFIG.SYS file. VDISK encountered a switch (/) but the character immediately following it was not an *E* for *extended memory*. MS-DOS loads VDISK and attempts to install VDISK in low (nonextended) memory. Either you have misspelled the */E* switch, or you have left a space between the / and the *E*. Edit and save your CONFIG.SYS file, and restart MS-DOS.

Memory allocation error
Cannot load COMMAND, system halted

ERROR: A program destroyed the area where MS-DOS keeps track of in-use and available memory. You must restart MS-DOS.

If this error occurs again with the same program, the program has a flaw. Use a backup copy of the program. If the problem persists, contact the dealer or program publisher.

Missing operating system

ERROR (start-up): The MS-DOS hard disk partition entry is marked as "bootable" (able to start MS-DOS), but the MS-DOS partition does not have a copy of MS-DOS on it. MS-DOS does not boot.

Start MS-DOS from a diskette. If you have existing files on the hard disk, back up the files. Issue FORMAT /S to put a copy of the operating system on the hard disk. If necessary, restore the files that you backed up.

No free file handles
Cannot start COMMAND, exiting

ERROR: MS-DOS could not load an additional copy of COMMAND.COM because no file handles (FILES=) were available.

Edit the CONFIG.SYS file on your start-up disk to increase the number of file handles (using the FILES command) by five. Restart MS-DOS and try the command again.

Non-System disk or disk error
Replace and strike any key when
ready

ERROR (start-up): Your diskette or hard disk does not
contain MS-DOS, or a read error occurred when you
started the system. MS-DOS does not boot.

If you are using a floppy disk system, put a bootable
diskette in drive A: and press a key.

The most frequent cause of this message on hard
disk systems is that you left a nonbootable diskette in
disk drive A: with the door closed. Open the door to disk
drive A: and press a key. MS- DOS will boot from the
hard disk.

Not enough memory

ERROR: The computer does not have enough free
RAM memory to execute the program or command.
If you loaded a resident program like PRINT,
GRAPHICS, SideKick, or ProKey, restart MS-DOS and
try the command again before loading any resident
program. If this method fails, remove any unneeded
device driver or RAM-disk software from the
CONFIG.SYS file and restart MS-DOS again. If this
option fails also, your computer does not have enough
memory for this command. You must increase your
RAM memory to run the command.

Out of environment space

WARNING: MS-DOS is unable to add to the
environment any more strings from the SET command.
The environment cannot be expanded. This error occurs
when you load a resident program, such as MODE,
PRINT, GRAPHICS, SideKick, or ProKey.

If you are running MS-DOS V3.1 or later, refer to the
SHELL command for information about expanding the

default space for the environment. MS-DOS V3.0 has no method to expand the environment.

Path not found

ERROR: A file or directory path you named does not exist. You may have misspelled the file name or directory name, or you omitted a path character (\) between directory names or between the final directory name and file name. Another possibility is that the file or directory does not exist where you specified. Check these possibilities and try again.

Path too long

ERROR: You have given a path name that exceeds the 63 character limit of MS-DOS. Either the name is too long, or you omitted a space between file names. Check the command line. If the phrasing is correct, you must change to a directory that is closer to the file you want and try the command again.

Program too big to fit in memory

ERROR: The computer does not have enough memory to load the program or command you invoked.

If you have any resident programs loaded (such as PRINT, GRAPHICS, or SideKick), restart MS-DOS and try the command again without loading the resident programs. If this message appears again, reduce the number of buffers (BUFFERS=) in the CONFIG.SYS file, eliminate unneeded device drivers or RAM-disk software, and restart MS-DOS again. If these actions do not solve the problem, your computer does not have enough RAM memory for the program or command. You must increase the amount of RAM memory in your computer to run this command.

Sector size too large in file filename

WARNING: The device driver is inconsistent. The device driver defined a particular sector size to MS-DOS but attempted to use a different size. Either the copy of the device driver is bad, or the device driver is incorrect. Copy a backup of the device driver to the boot diskette and then reboot MS-DOS. If the message appears again, the device driver is incorrect. If you wrote the driver, correct the error. If you purchased the program, contact the dealer or software publisher.

Sharing violation

WARNING: With the file-sharing program (SHARE.EXE) loaded, you or one of your programs attempted to access a file by using a sharing mode not allowed at this time. Another program or computer has temporary control over the file.

You will see the message Abort, Retry, Ignore. Choose R for Retry several times. If the problem persists, choose A for Abort. If you abort, however, any data currently being manipulated by the program is lost.

Syntax error

ERROR: You phrased a command improperly by (1) omitting needed information; (2) giving extraneous information; (3) putting an extra space in a file name or path name; or (4) using an incorrect switch. Check the command line for these possibilities and try the command again.

Too many block devices

WARNING (start-up): There are too many DEVICE directives in your CONFIG.SYS file. MS-DOS continues to start but does not install any additional device drivers.

MS-DOS can handle only 26 block devices. The block devices created by the DEVICE directives plus the number of block devices automatically created by MS-DOS exceeds this number. Remove any unnecessary DEVICE directives in your CONFIG.SYS file and restart MS-DOS.

Top level process aborted, cannot continue

ERROR (start-up): COMMAND.COM or another MS-DOS command detected a disk error, and you chose the A (abort) option. MS-DOS cannot finish starting itself, and the system halts.

Try to start MS-DOS again. If the error recurs, use a floppy diskette (if starting from the hard disk) or a different floppy diskette (if starting from floppy diskettes) to start MS-DOS. After it has started, use the SYS command to put another copy of the operating system on the disk, and copy COMMAND.COM to the disk. If MS-DOS reports an error during the copying, the disk or diskette is bad. Either reformat or retire the floppy diskette, or back-up and reformat the hard disk.

Unable to create directory

ERROR: Either you or a program has attempted to create a directory, and one of the following has occurred: (1) a directory by the same name already exists; (2) a file by the same name already exists; (3) you are adding a directory to the root directory, and the root directory is full; or (4) the directory name has illegal characters or is a device name.

Do a DIR of the disk. Make sure that no file or directory already exists with the same name. If adding the directory to the root directory, remove or move (copy, then erase) any unneeded files or directives. Check the spelling of the directory and ensure that the command is properly phrased.

Unrecognized command in CONFIG.SYS

WARNING (start-up): MS-DOS detected an improperly phrased directive in CONFIG.SYS. The directive is ignored, and MS-DOS continues to start; but MS-DOS does not indicate the incorrect line. Examine the CONFIG.SYS file, looking for improperly phrased or incorrect directives. Edit the line, save the file, and restart MS-DOS.

MS-DOS Device Error Messages

When MS-DOS detects an error while reading or writing to disk drives or other devices, one of the following message appears:

> *type* error reading *device*

> *type* error writing *device*

type is the type of error, and *device* is the device at fault. If the device is a floppy disk drive, do not remove the diskette from the drive. Refer to the possible causes and corrective actions described in this section, which lists the types of error messages that may appear.

Bad call format

A device driver was given a requested header with an incorrect length. The problem is the applications software making the call.

Bad command

The device driver issued an invalid or unsupported command to the device. The problem may be with the device driver software or with other software trying to use the device driver.

Bad format call

The device driver at fault passed an incorrect header length to MS-DOS. If you wrote this device driver, you must rewrite it to correct the problem. For a purchased program, contact the dealer or publisher who sold you the driver.

Bad unit

An invalid sub-unit number was passed to the device driver. The problem may be with the device driver software or with other software trying to use the device driver. Contact the dealer who sold you the device driver.

Data

MS-DOS could not correctly read or write the data. Usually the disk has developed a defective spot.

Drive not ready

An error occurred while MS-DOS tried to read or write to the disk drive. For floppy disk drives, the drive door may be open, the micro diskette may not be inserted, or the diskette may not be formatted. For hard disk drives, the drive may not be properly prepared or you may have a hardware problem.

FCB unavailable

With the file-sharing program (SHARE.EXE) loaded, a program that uses the MS-DOS V1 method of file handling attempted to open concurrently more file control blocks than were specified with the FCBS command.

Use the Abort option (see the end of the section).
Increase the value of the FCBS CONFIG.SYS command
(usually by four) and reboot the system. If the message
appears again, increase the number again and reboot.

General failure

This is a catchall error message not covered elsewhere.
The error usually occurs when you use an unformatted
diskette or hard disk, or when you leave the disk drive
door open.

Lock violation

With the file-sharing program (SHARE.EXE) or
network software loaded, one of your programs
attempted to access a file that is locked. Your best
choice is Retry. Then try Abort. If you choose A,
however, any data in memory is lost.

No paper

The printer is either out of paper or not turned on.

Non-DOS disk

The FAT has invalid information. This diskette is
unusable. You can Abort and run CHKDSK on the
diskette to see whether any corrective action is possible.
If CHKDSK fails, your other alternative is to reformat
the diskette. Reformatting, however, will destroy any
remaining information on the diskette. If you use more
than one operating system, the diskette has probably
been formatted under the operating system you're using
and should not be reformatted.

Not ready

The device is not ready and cannot receive or transmit
data. Check the connections, make sure that the power is
on, and check to see whether the device is ready.

Read fault

MS-DOS was unable to read the data, usually from a hard disk or diskette. Check the disk drive doors and be sure that the diskette is inserted properly.

Sector not found

The disk drive was unable to locate the sector on the diskette or hard disk platter. This error is usually the result of a defective spot on the disk or of defective drive electronics. Some copy-protection schemes also use this method (a defective spot) to prevent unauthorized duplication of the diskette.

Seek

The disk drive could not locate the proper track on the diskette or hard disk platter. This error is usually the result of a defective spot on the diskette or hard disk platter, an unformatted disk, or drive electronics problems.

Sharing violation

With the file-sharing program (SHARE.EXE) or network software loaded, your programs attempted to access a file by using a sharing mode not specified for that file. Your best response is Retry; if that doesn't work, try Abort.

Write fault

MS-DOS could not write the data to this device. Perhaps you inserted the diskette improperly, or you left the disk drive door open. Another possibility is an electronics failure in the floppy or hard disk drive. The most frequent cause is a bad spot on the diskette.

Write protect

The diskette is write-protected.

Note: One of the previously listed messages (usually Data, Read fault, or Write fault) appears when you are using a double-sided diskette in a single-sided disk drive or a 9-sector diskette (V2 and later) with a version of MS-DOS V1. MS-DOS will display one of these error messages followed by the line

```
Abort, Retry, Ignore?
```

If you press A for Abort, MS-DOS ends the program that requested the read or write condition. Typing R for Retry causes MS-DOS to try the operation again. If you press I for Ignore, MS-DOS skips the operation, and the program continues. However, some data may be lost when Ignore is used.

The order of preference, unless stated differently under the message, is R, A, and I. You should retry the operation at least twice. If the condition persists, you must decide whether to abort the program or ignore the error. If you ignore the error, data may be lost. If you abort, data still being processed by the program and not yet written to the disk will be lost. Remember that I is the least desirable option and that A should be used after Retry has failed at least two times.

DOS Survival Guide

Note: An asterisk (*) designates a CONFIG.SYS directive.

To   *Use*

Analyze a disk   CHKDSK
Automatically find files   APPEND, PATH
Automatically run a
  file at startup   AUTOEXEC.BAT
Print from the background   PRINT
Back up files   BACKUP, COPY, XCOPY
Back up disks   BACKUP, DISKCOPY
Change a code page   CHCP, KEYB, MODE
Change the active display   MODE
Change the baud rate   MODE
Change the console   CTTY
Change the current
  directory   CHDIR (CD)
Change the current disk
  drive   d:
Change disk buffers   BUFFERS*
Change the disk label   LABEL
Change the environment   SET
Change file attributes   ATTRIB
Change a file name   RENAME (REN)
Change/set location of
  the command interpreter   SHELL*
Change program input   <
Change program output   >,>>
Clear the video display   CLS
Combine disks   JOIN
Combine files   COPY
Compare diskettes   DISKCOMP
Compare files   COMP
Concatenate files   COPY
Connect disk drives   JOIN
Control Ctrl-Break   BREAK, BREAK*
Control verification of files   VERIFY
Copy diskettes   DISKCOPY,COPY, XC(

Copy backup files	RESTORE
Copy files	COPY, REPLACE, XCOPY
Create a subdirectory	MKDIR (MD)
Display available RAM	CHKDSK
Display the current code page	CHCP, MODE
Display the date	DATE
Display the version of DOS	VER
Display environmental variables	SET
Display contents of a file	MORE, TYPE
Display a list of directories	CHKDSK /V, TREE
Display a list of files	DIR, CHKDSK /V, TREE /F
Display national-language characters	CHCP, GRAFTABL, KEYB, MODE
Display the time	TIME
Display the volume label	VOL, LABEL, DIR, CHKDSK
Erase a character	Backspace
Erase a directory	RMDIR (RD)
Erase a disk label	LABEL
Erase files	DEL, ERASE
Ignore a line	Esc
Execute several DOS cmds with one command	Batch file
Find disk free space	CHKDSK, DIR
Find a file	CHKDSK /V, TREE /F
Find a word or phrase in a file	FIND
Freeze the video display	Ctrl-NumLock, Pause
Load file-sharing software	SHARE
Pause the display	Ctrl-Num Lock, Pause, Ctrl-S
Pipe output between programs	|
Place DOS on a disk	SYS, FORMAT /S
Prepare a disk	FORMAT, FDISK
Print graphics	GRAPHICS
Print the display	Shift-PrintSc, GRAPHICS

Print on the display and the printer	Ctrl-PrintSc
Print a file	PRINT, >,>>
Reassign disk drives	ASSIGN, JOIN, SUBST
Reassign printers	MODE
Restore backup files	RESTORE
Repair a file	RECOVER
Repair a disk	RECOVER, CHKDSK
Remove a directory	RMDIR (RD)
Remove files	DEL, ERASE
Run a program	program_name
Set alternative directories for programs	PATH
Set alternative directories for data files	APPEND
Set the country code	COUNTRY*
Set/change a code page	MODE, KEYB
Set/change checks on file writing	VERIFY
Set/change communications ports	MODE
Set/change displays	MODE
Set/change an environmental variable	SET
Set/change printers	MODE
Set/change internal stacks	STACKS*
Set/change the system date	DATE
Set/change the system prompt	PROMPT
Set/change the system time	TIME
Sort a file	SORT
Speed DOS	BUFFERS*, FASTOPEN
Stop a running program	Ctrl-Break, Ctrl-C
Stop a running program and reset the computer	Ctrl-Alt-Del
Unfreeze the video display	Any key
Update files	REPLACE
Use a different disk drive	d:, ASSIGN, SUBST
Use a new device	DEVICE*
Use a subdirectory in place of a disk	SUBST